Sunsets from Florida's Nature Coast

The Changing Skies over the Gulf of Mexico

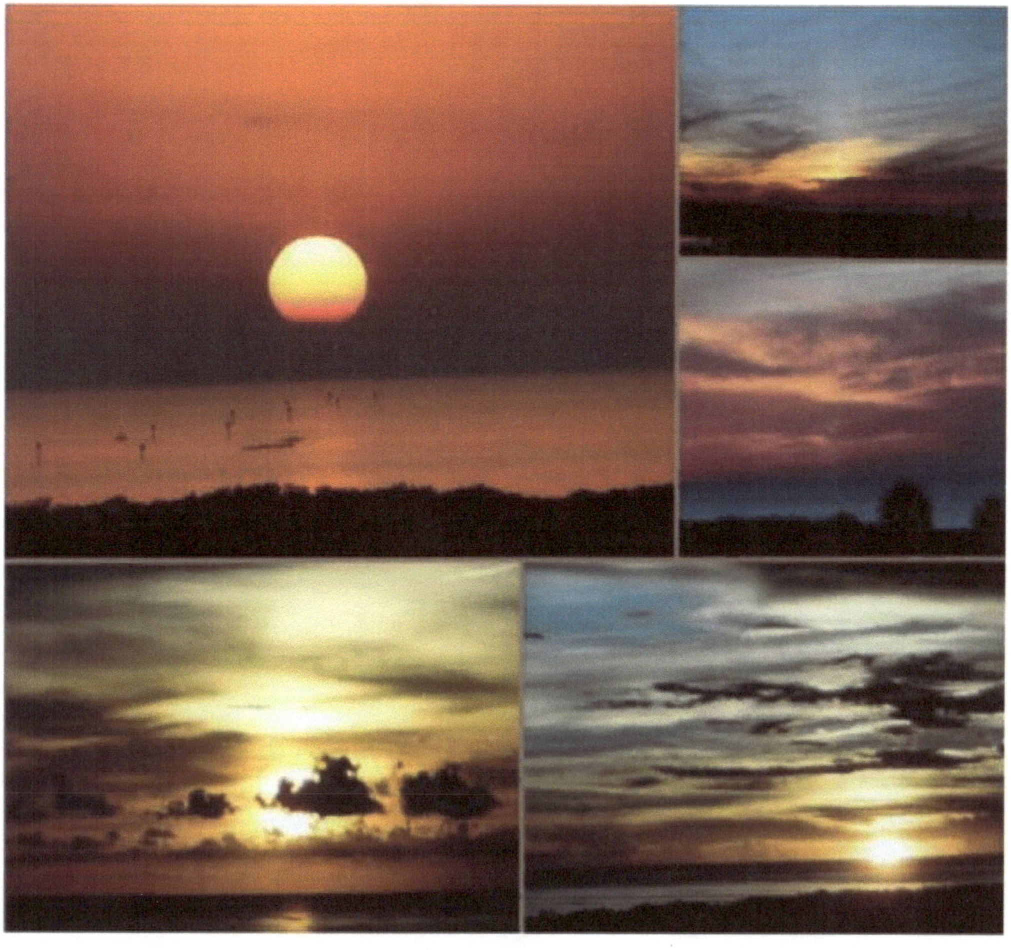

By Marilyn LaFiura

The author personally, photographed
all of the photos in this book.

They were all taken in Pasco County, Florida
along the Nature Coast.

The author was enthralled with the ever-changing
sky over the Gulf of Mexico! Every night resulted in a
very different photo, even though all the photos
were taken from the exact same location each night!

If you would like to purchase any of the photos in
this book, please contact me at
marilynl1009@gmail.com

Most photos are available for purchase in various sizes

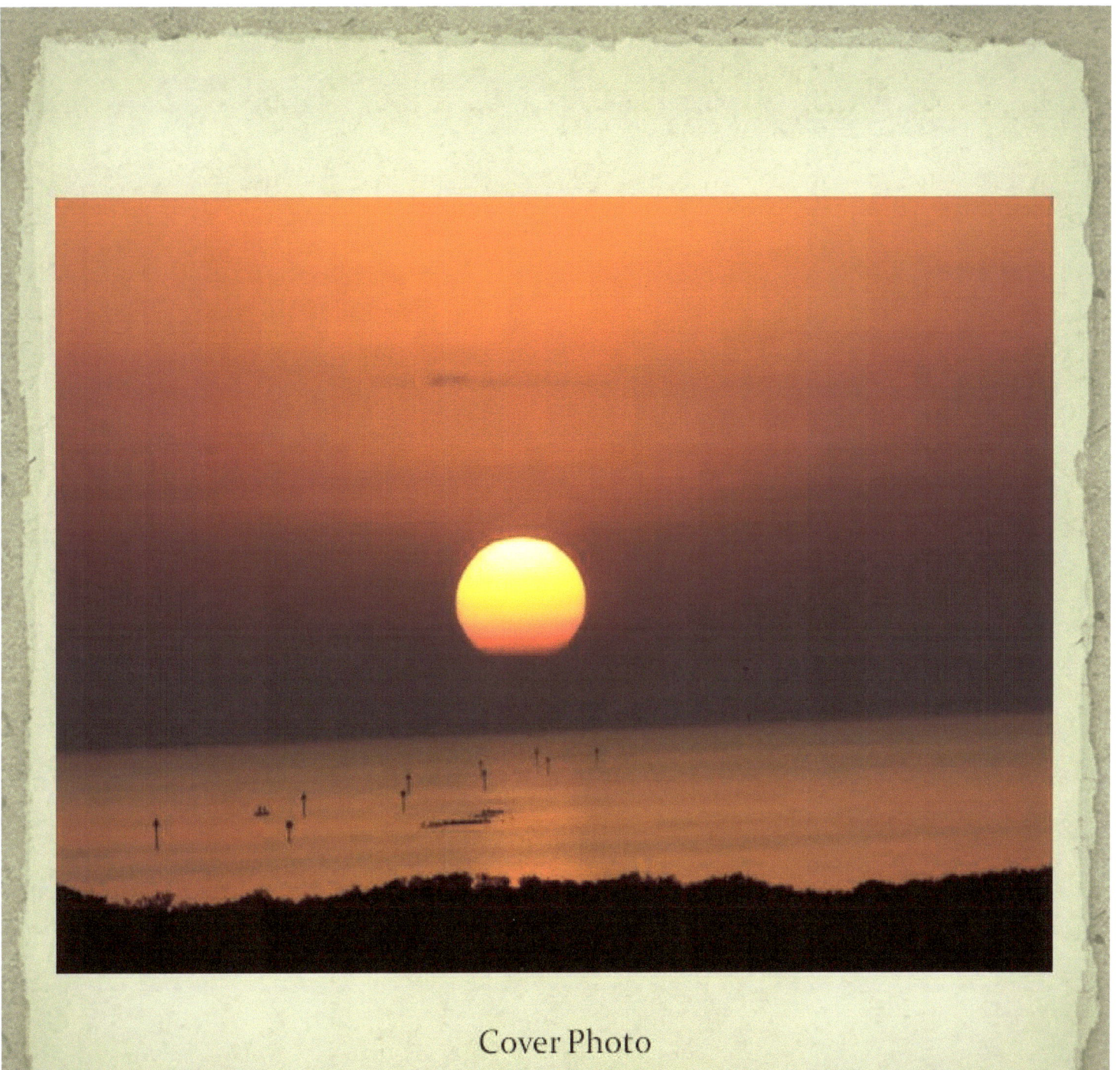
Cover Photo

Cover Photo

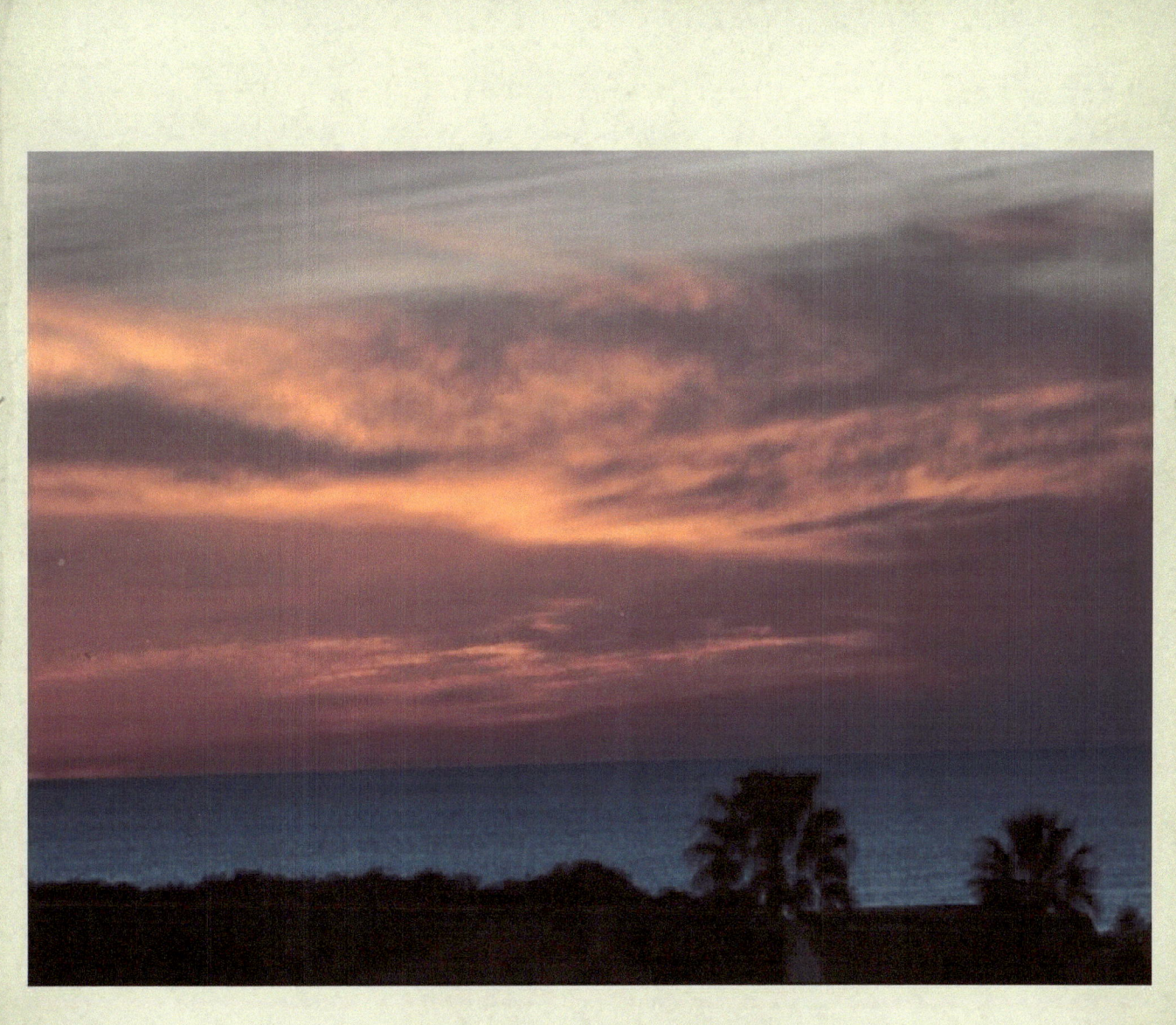

Cover Photo

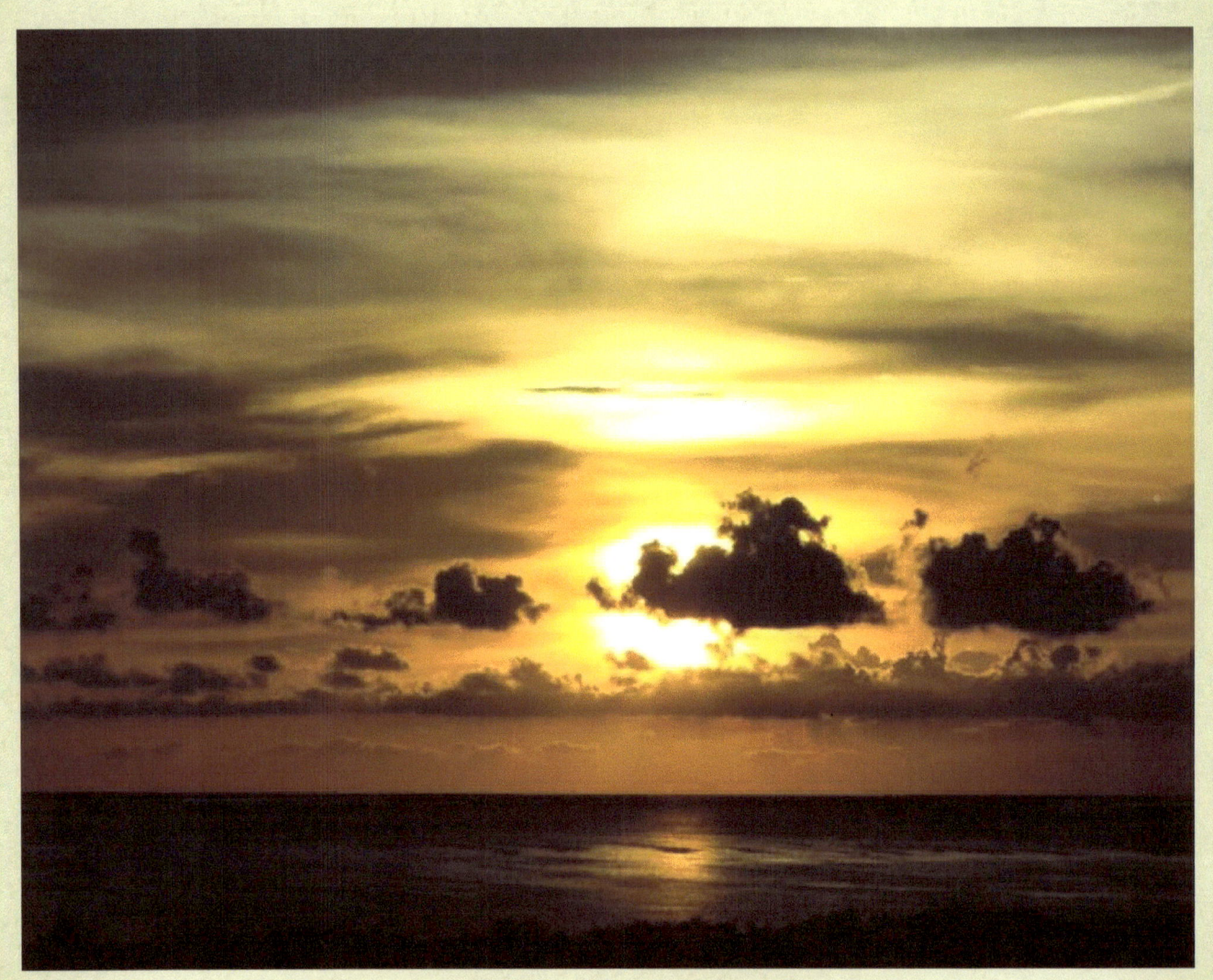

Cover Photo

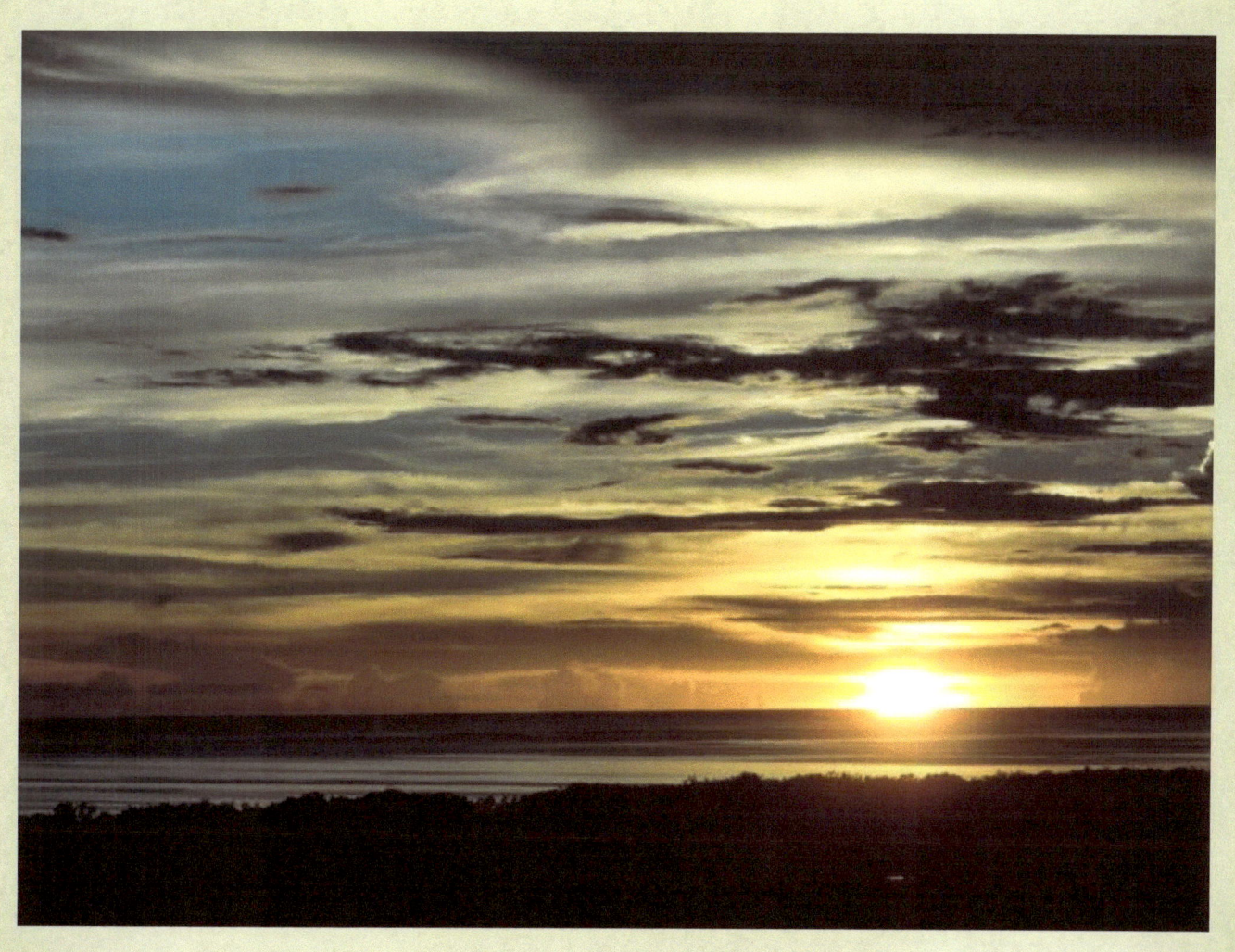

Cover Photo

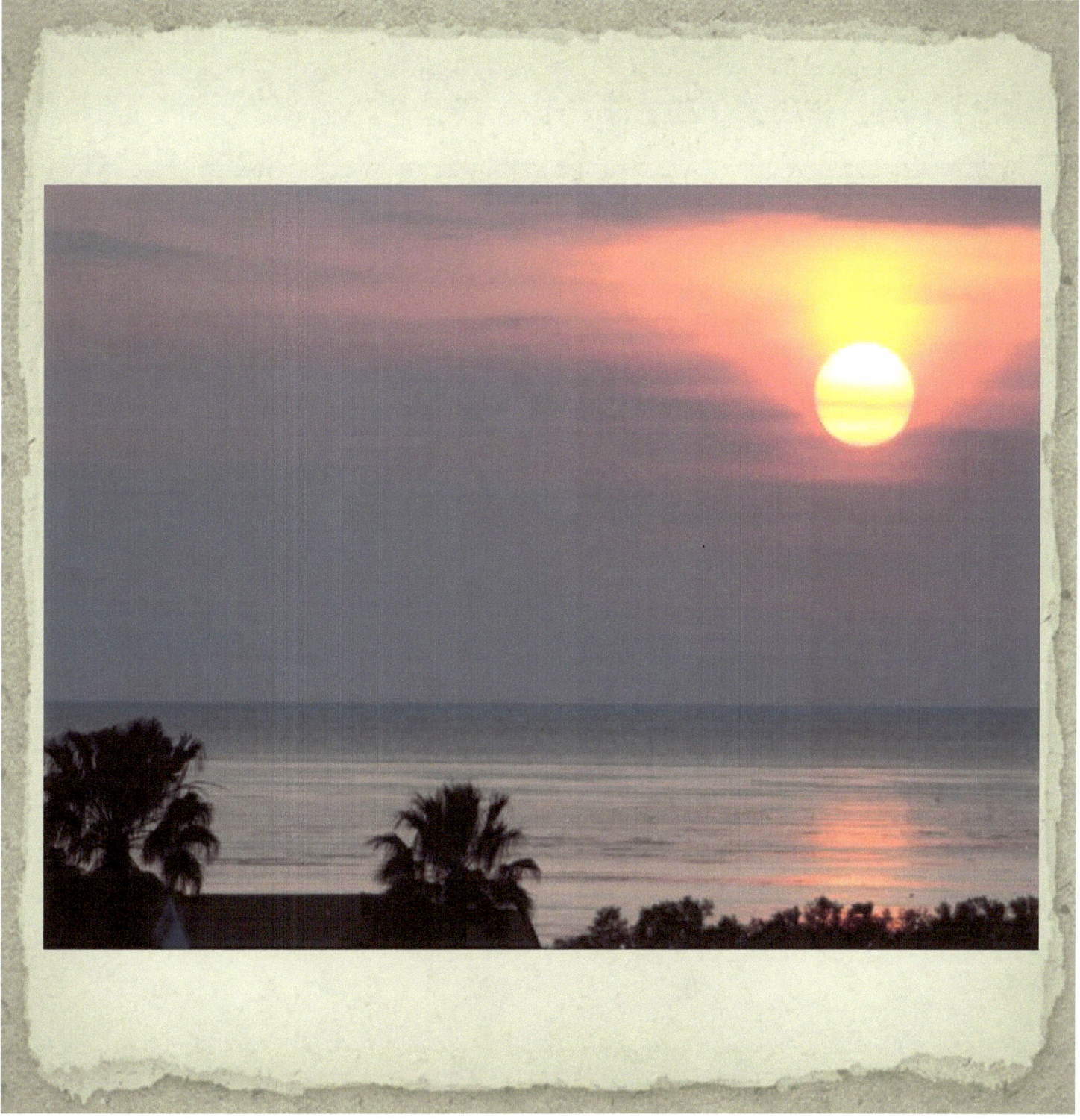

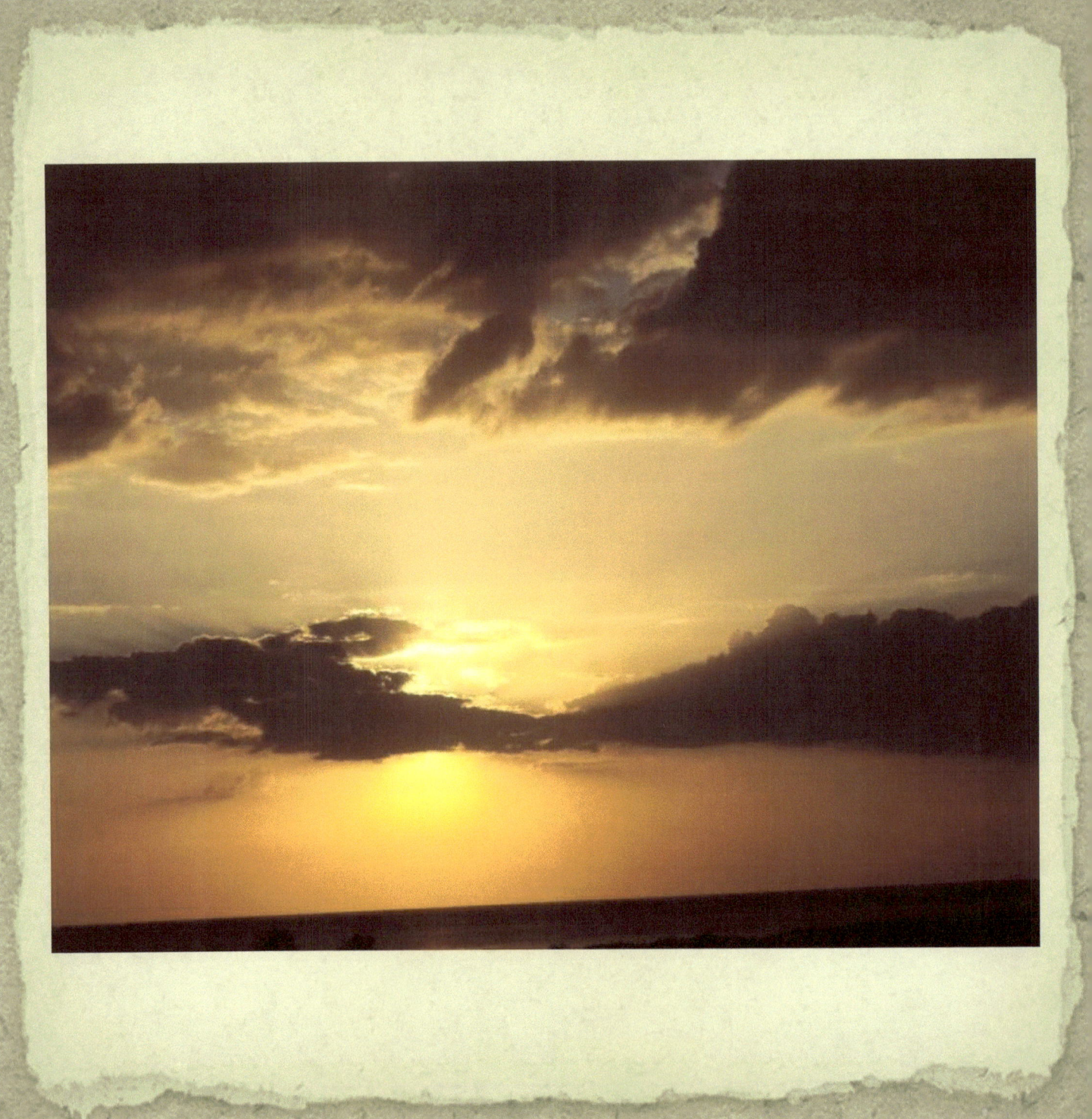

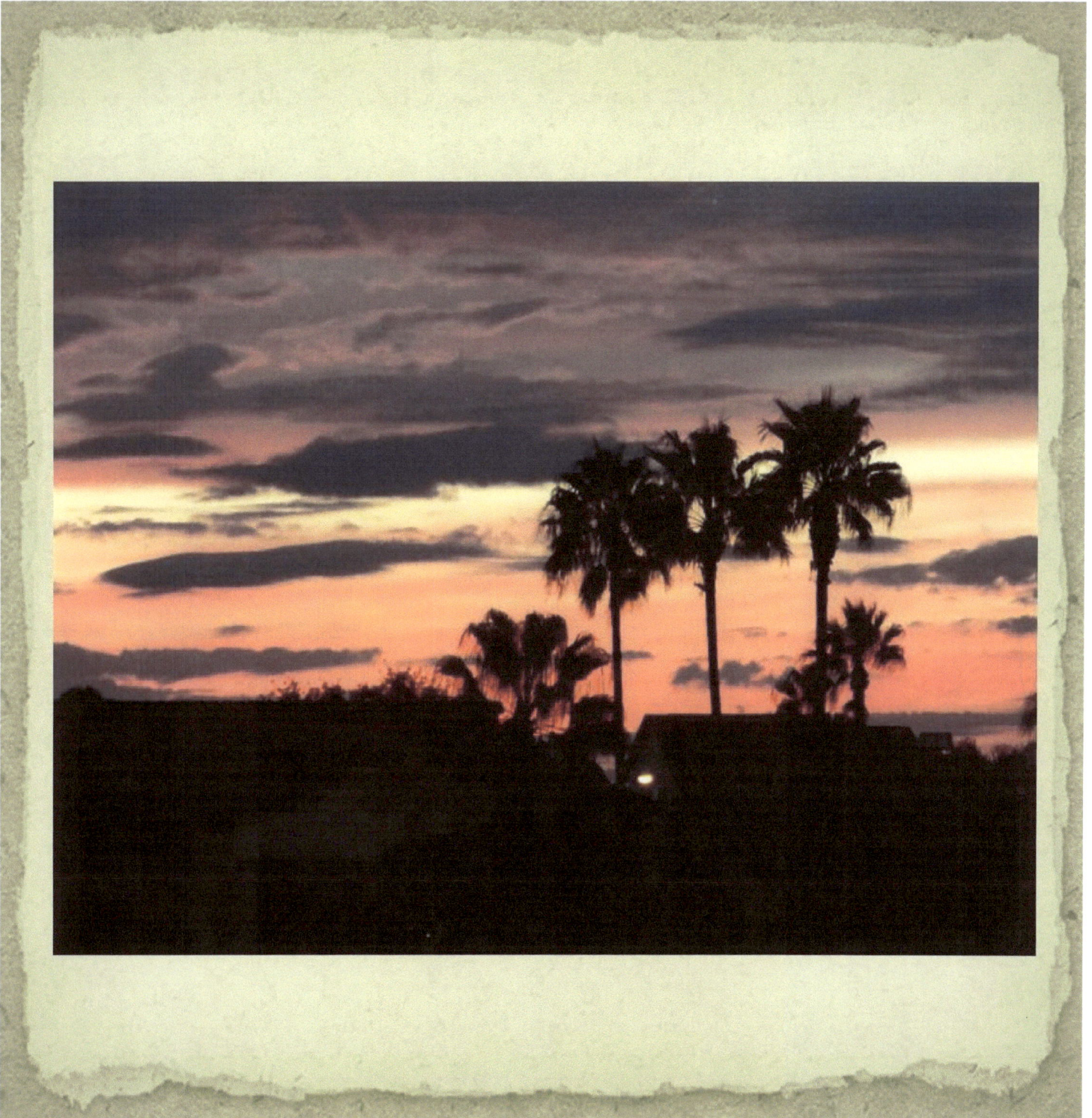

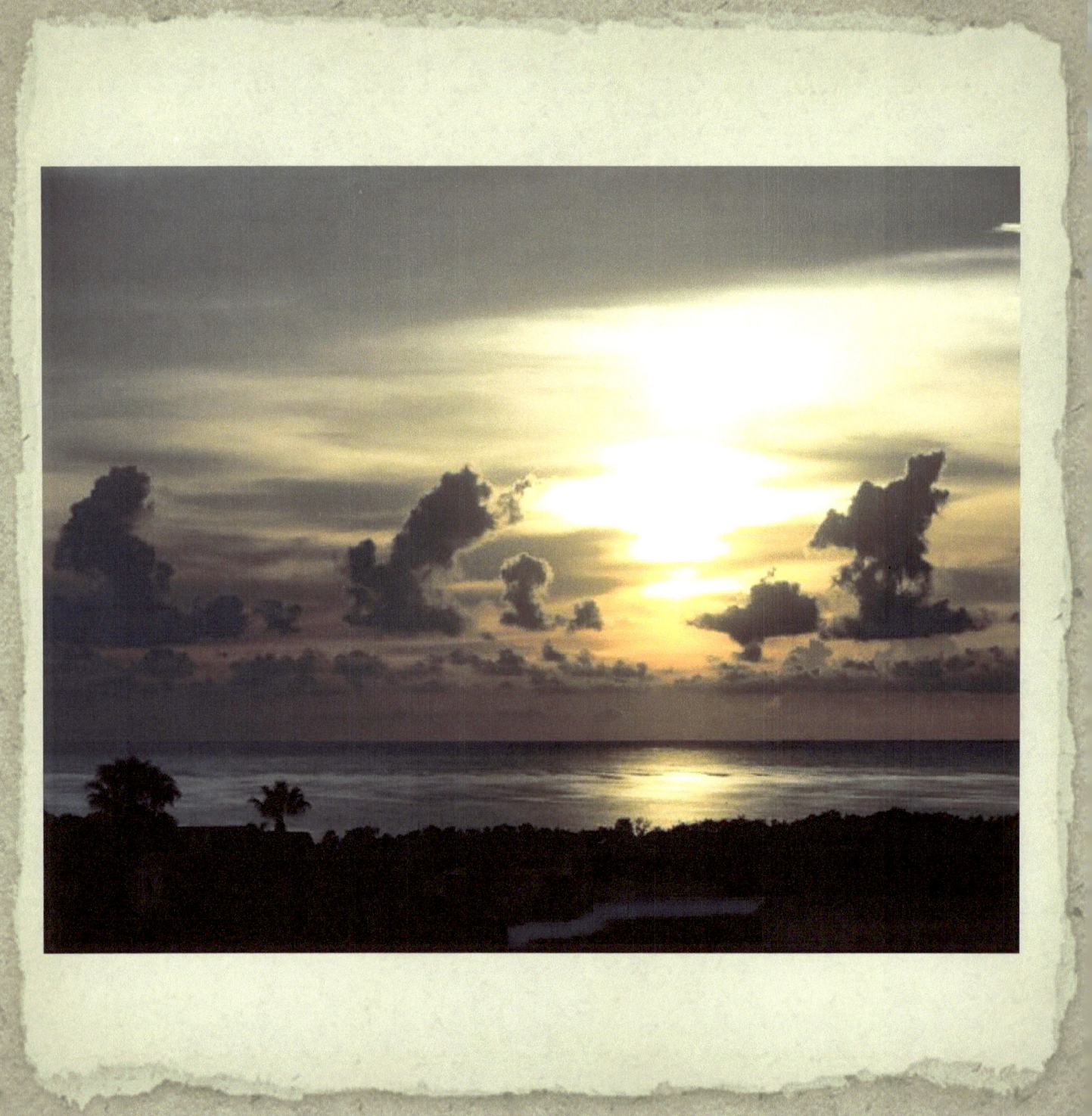

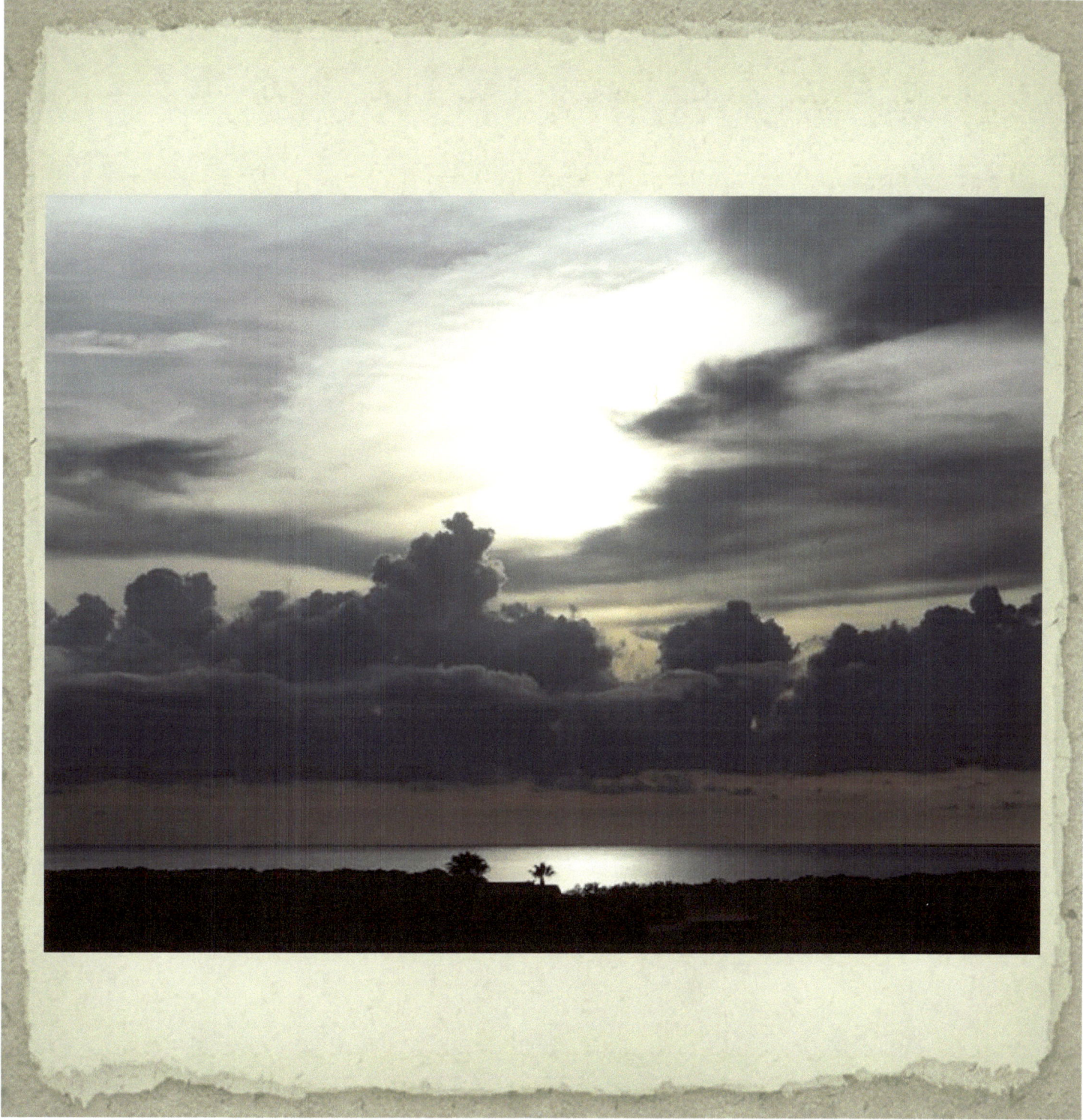

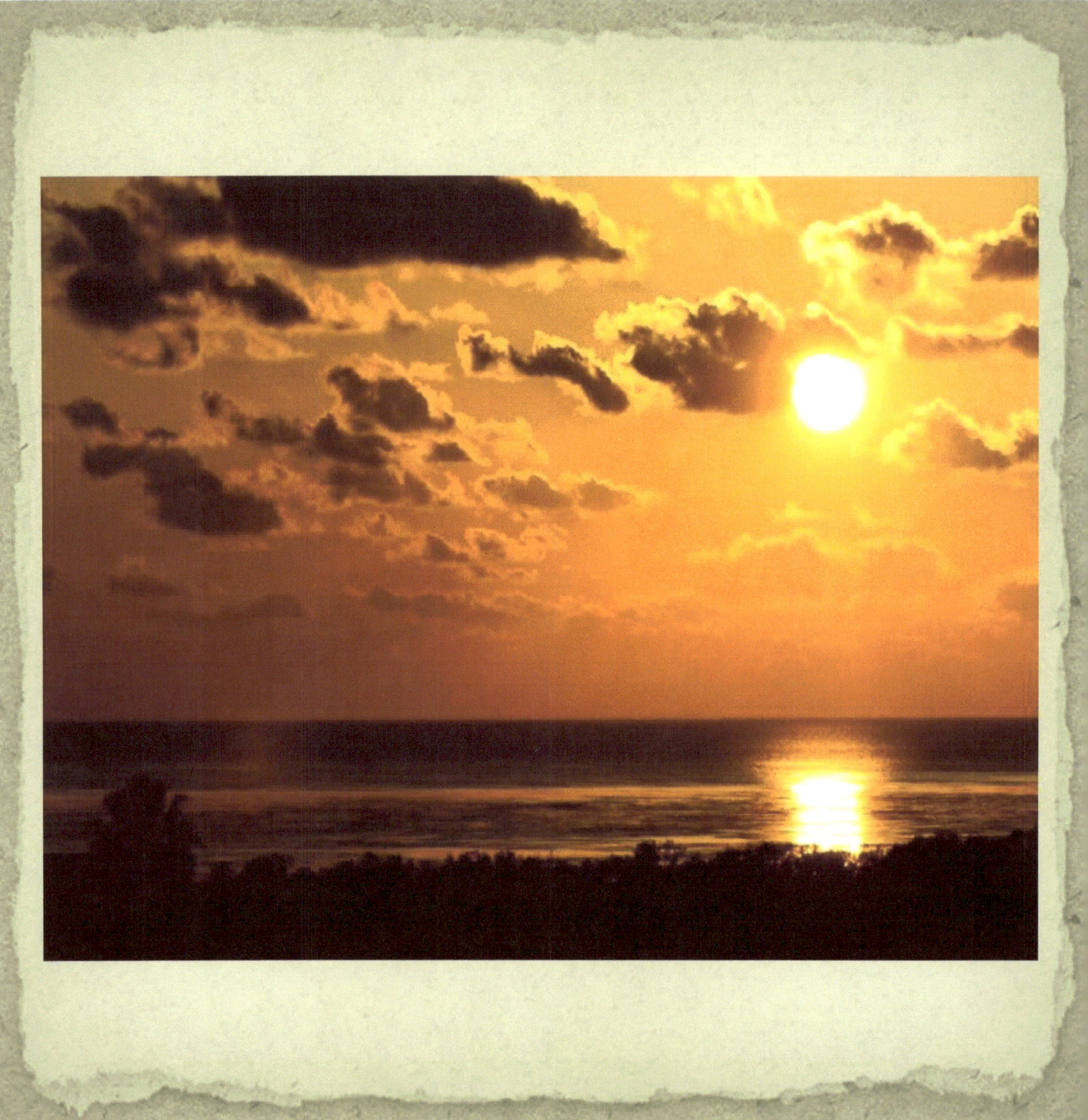

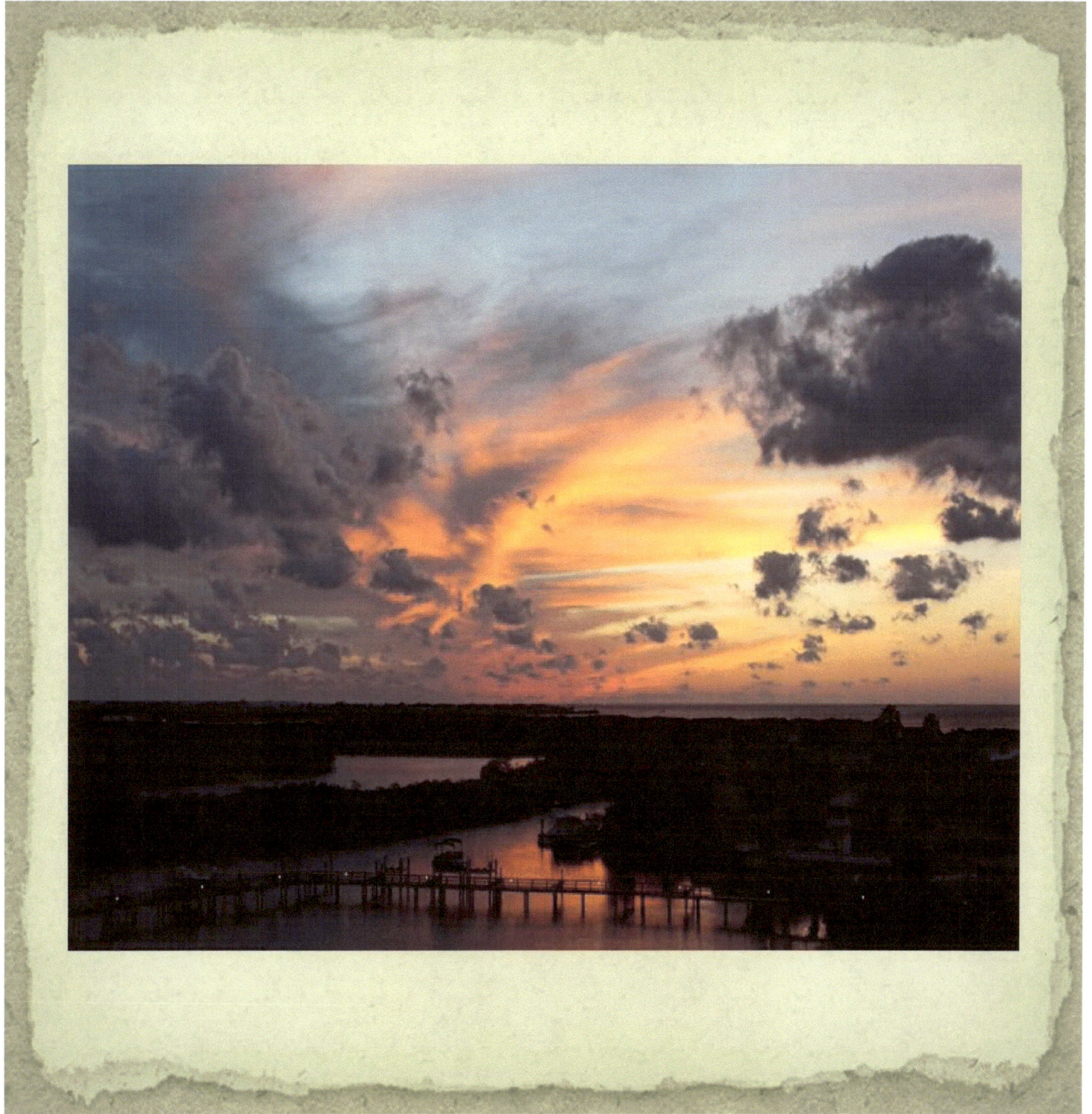

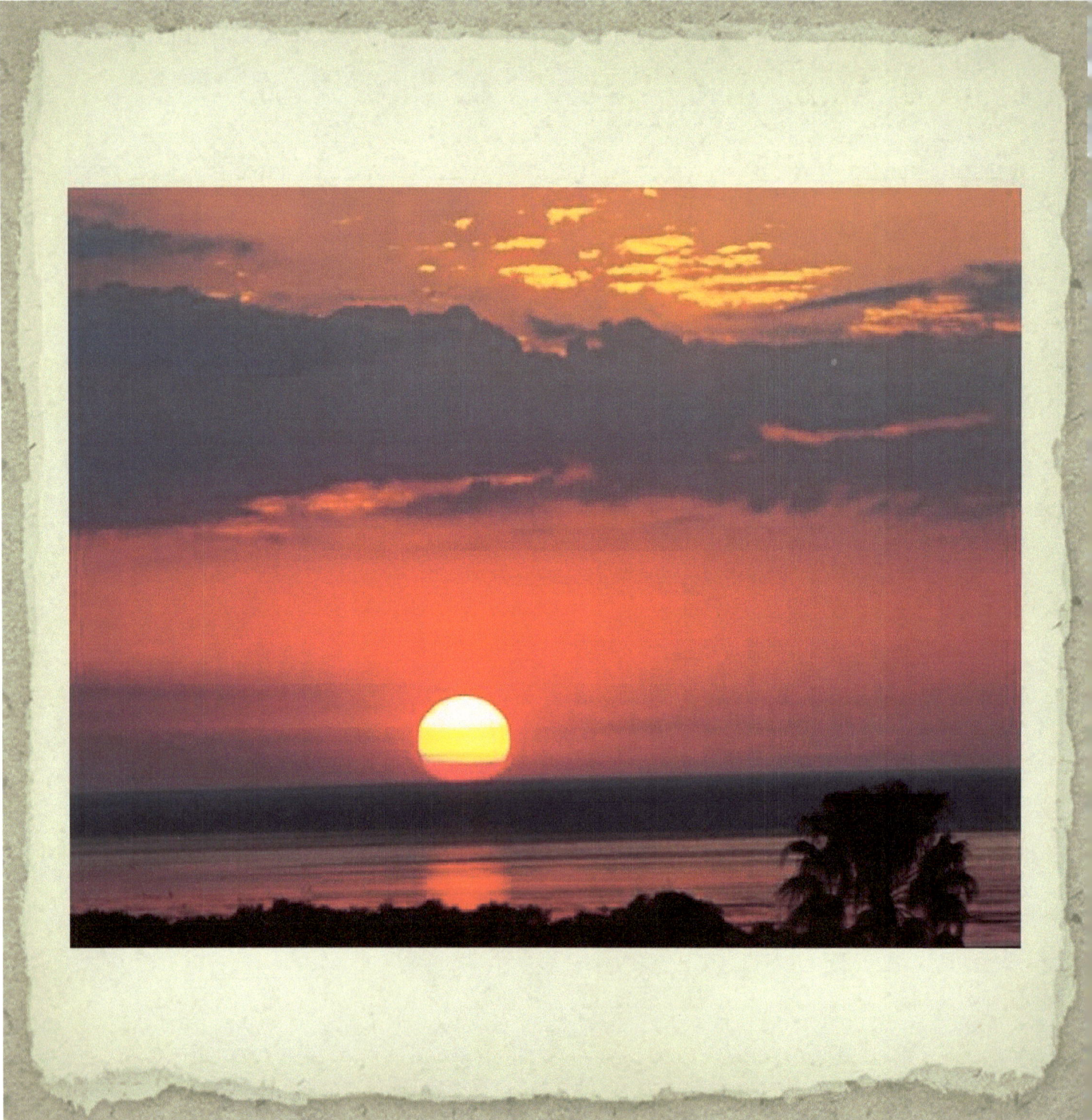

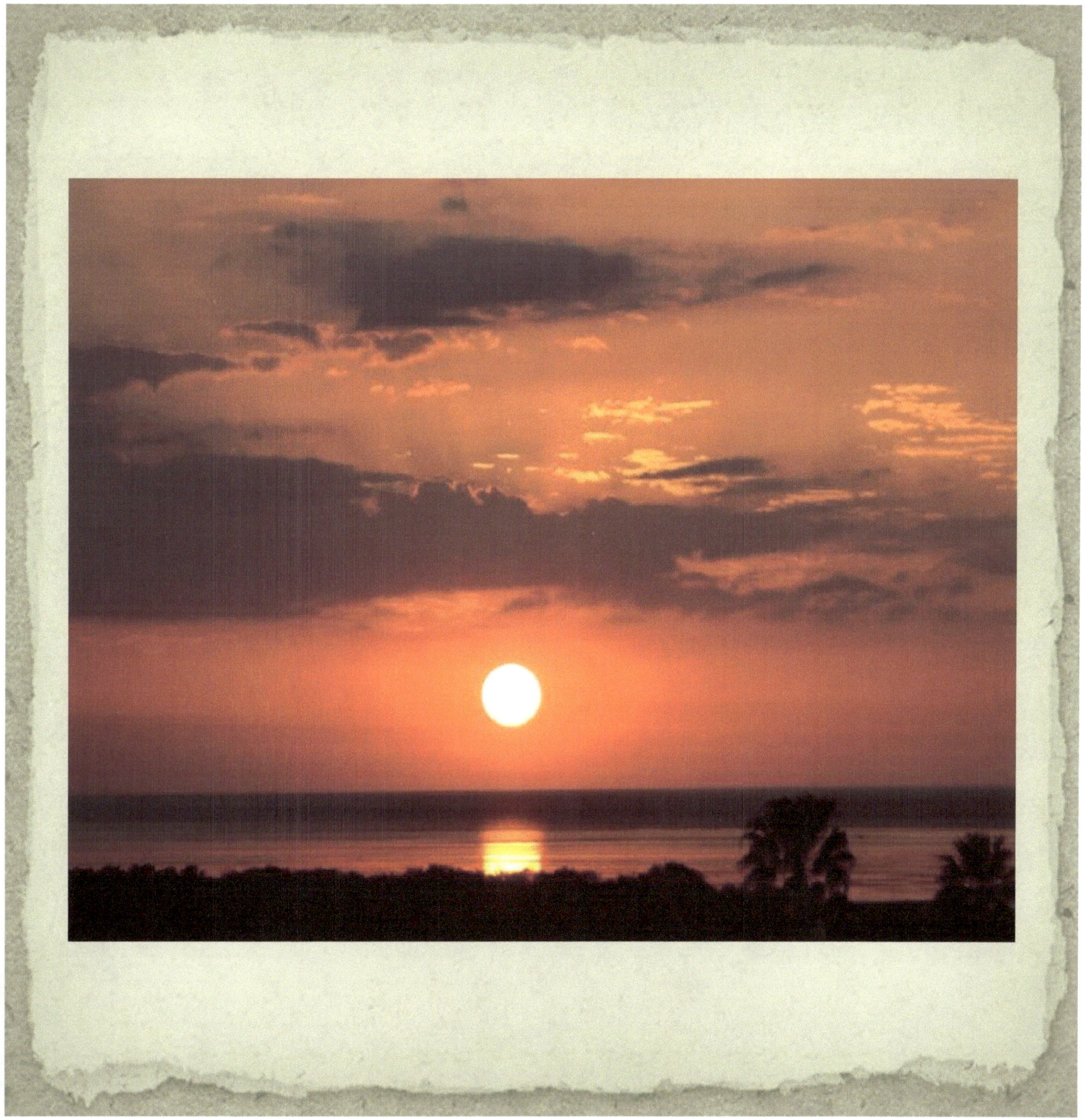

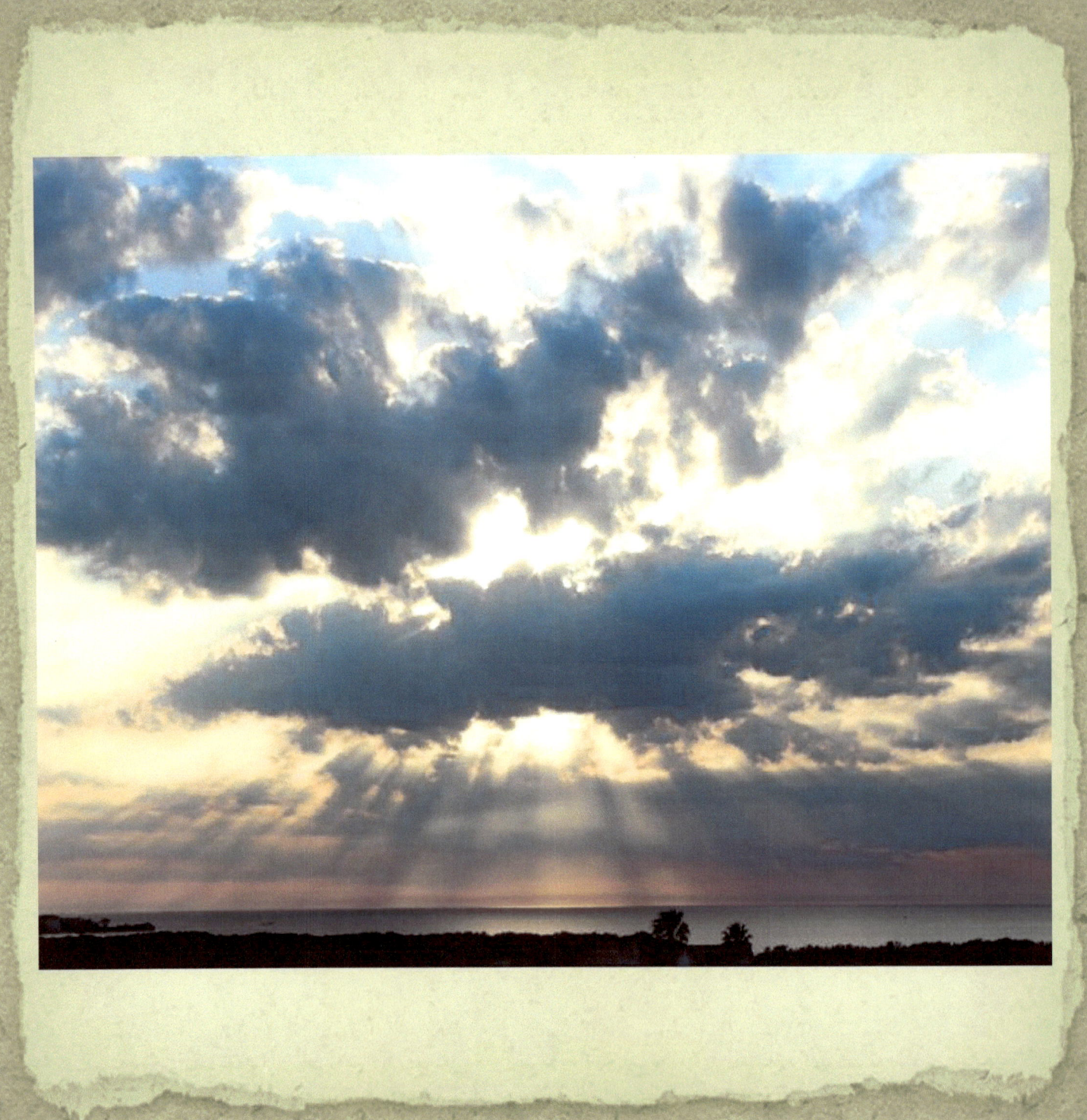

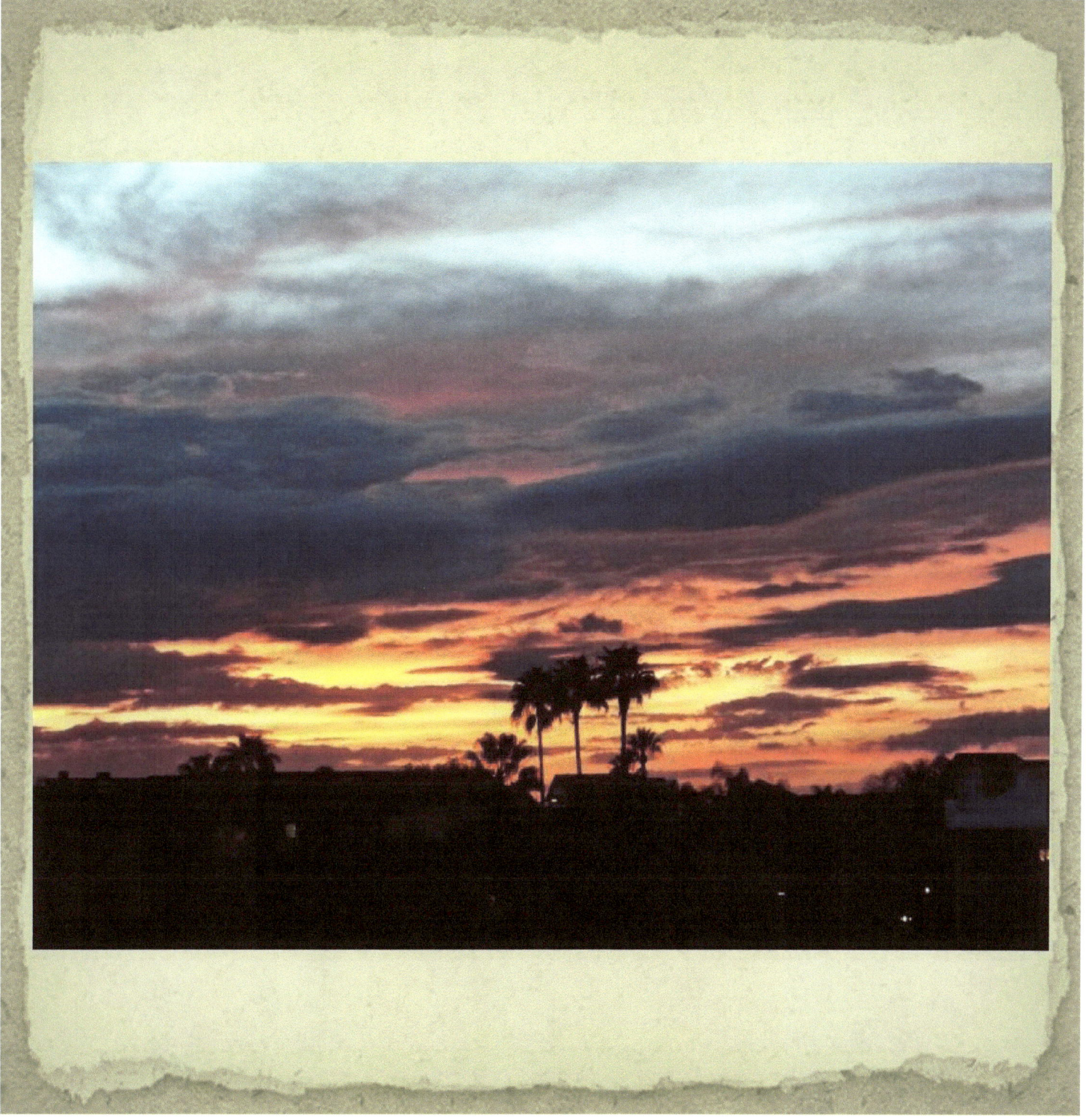

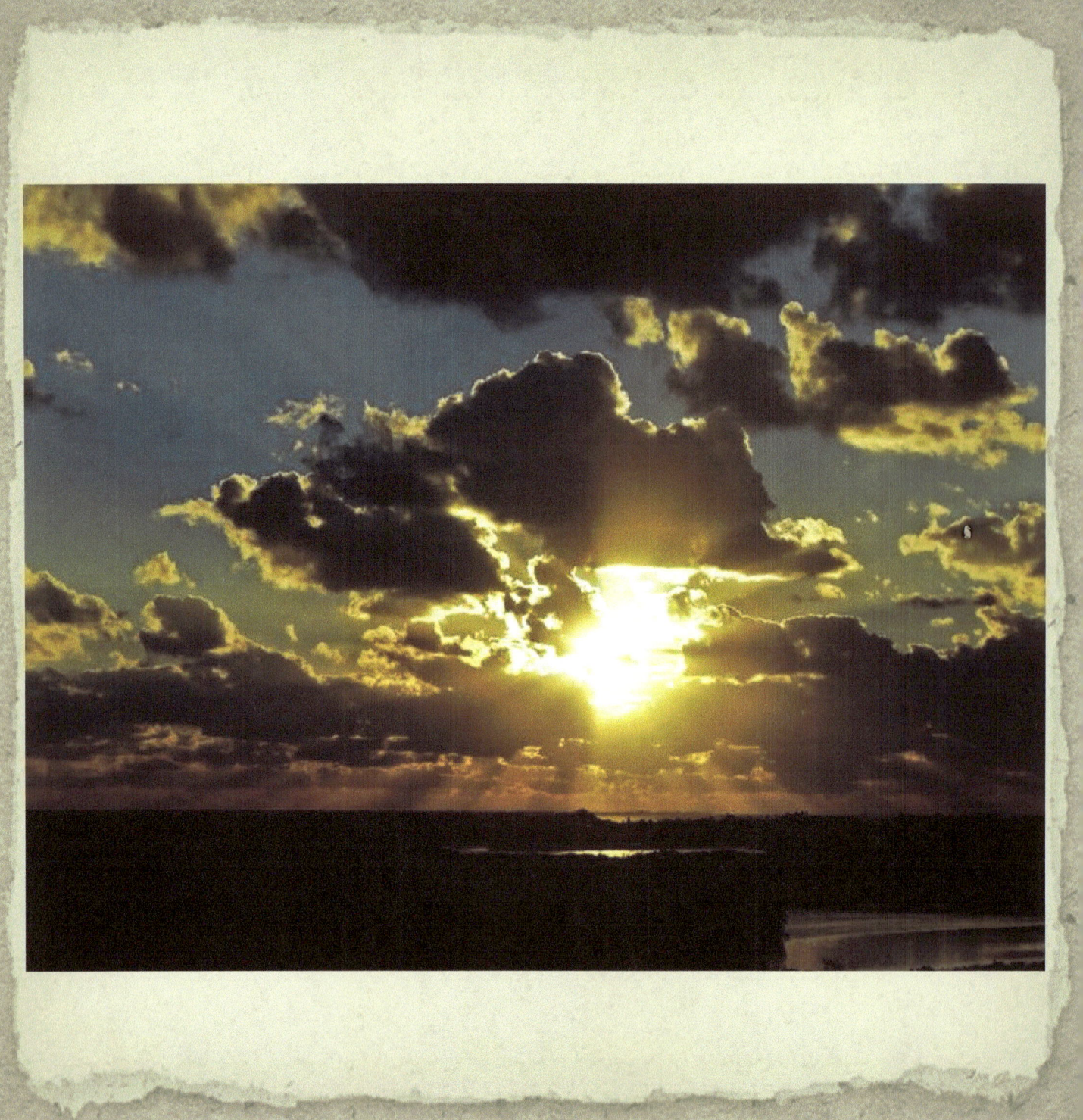

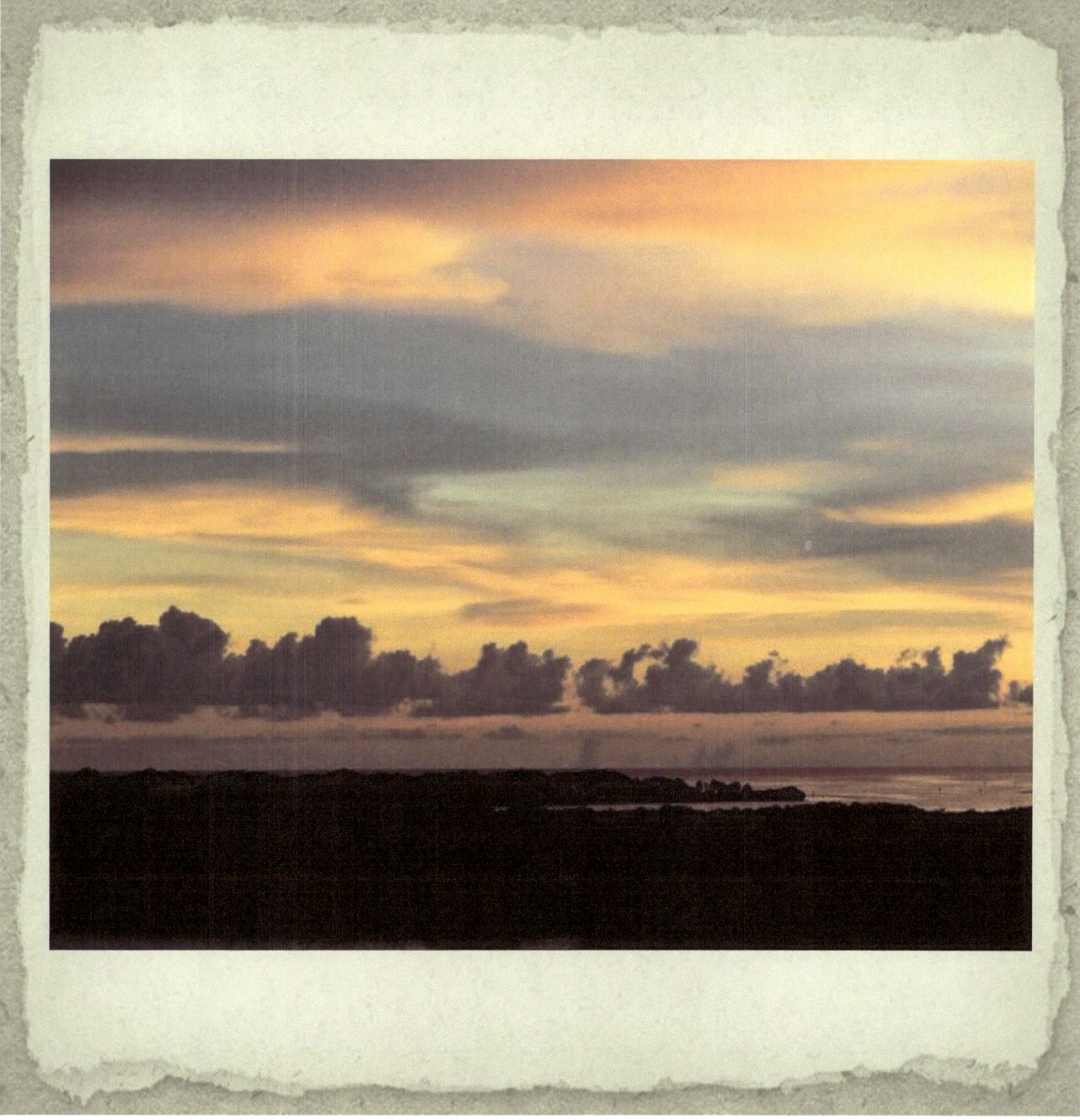

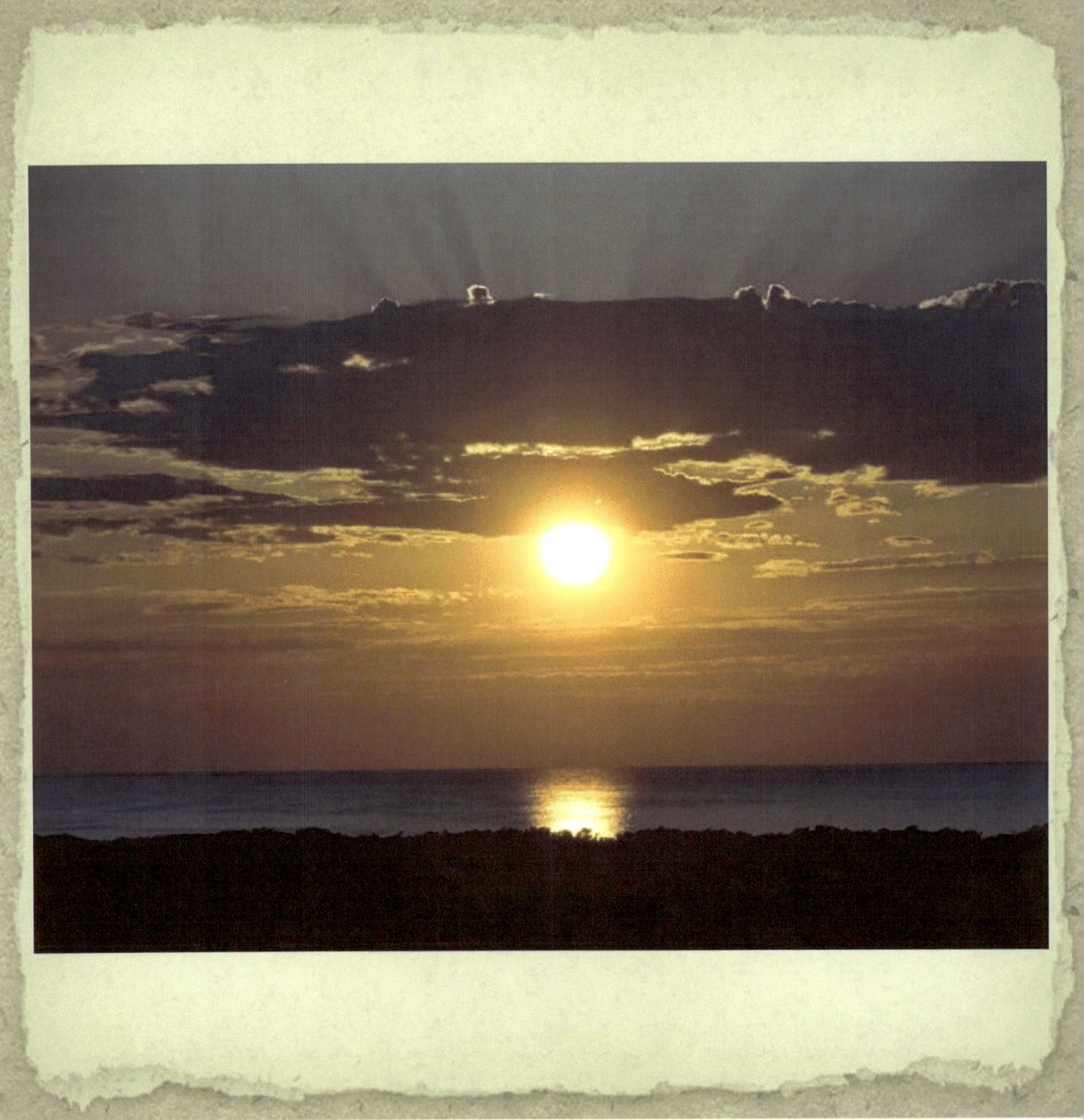

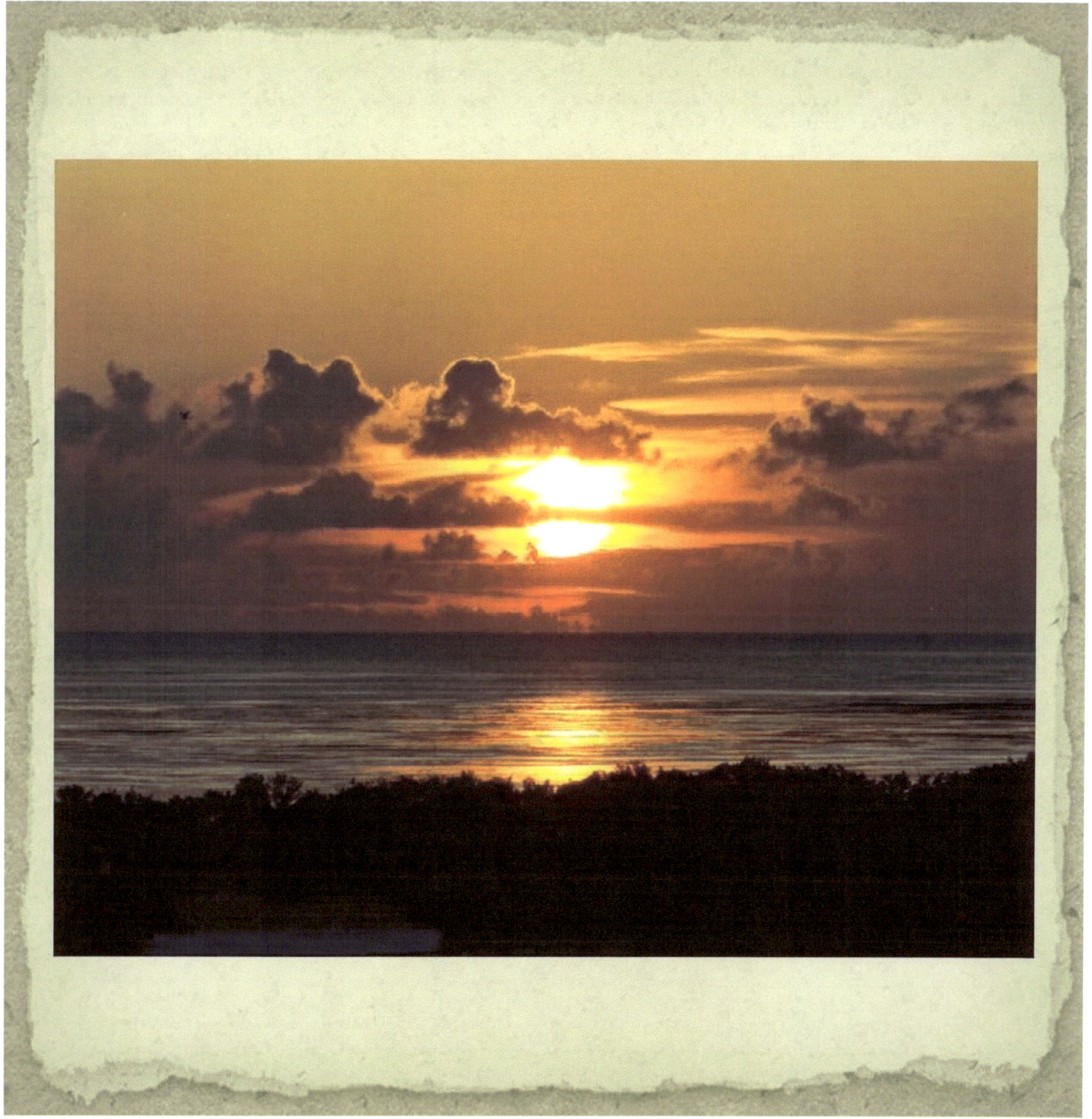

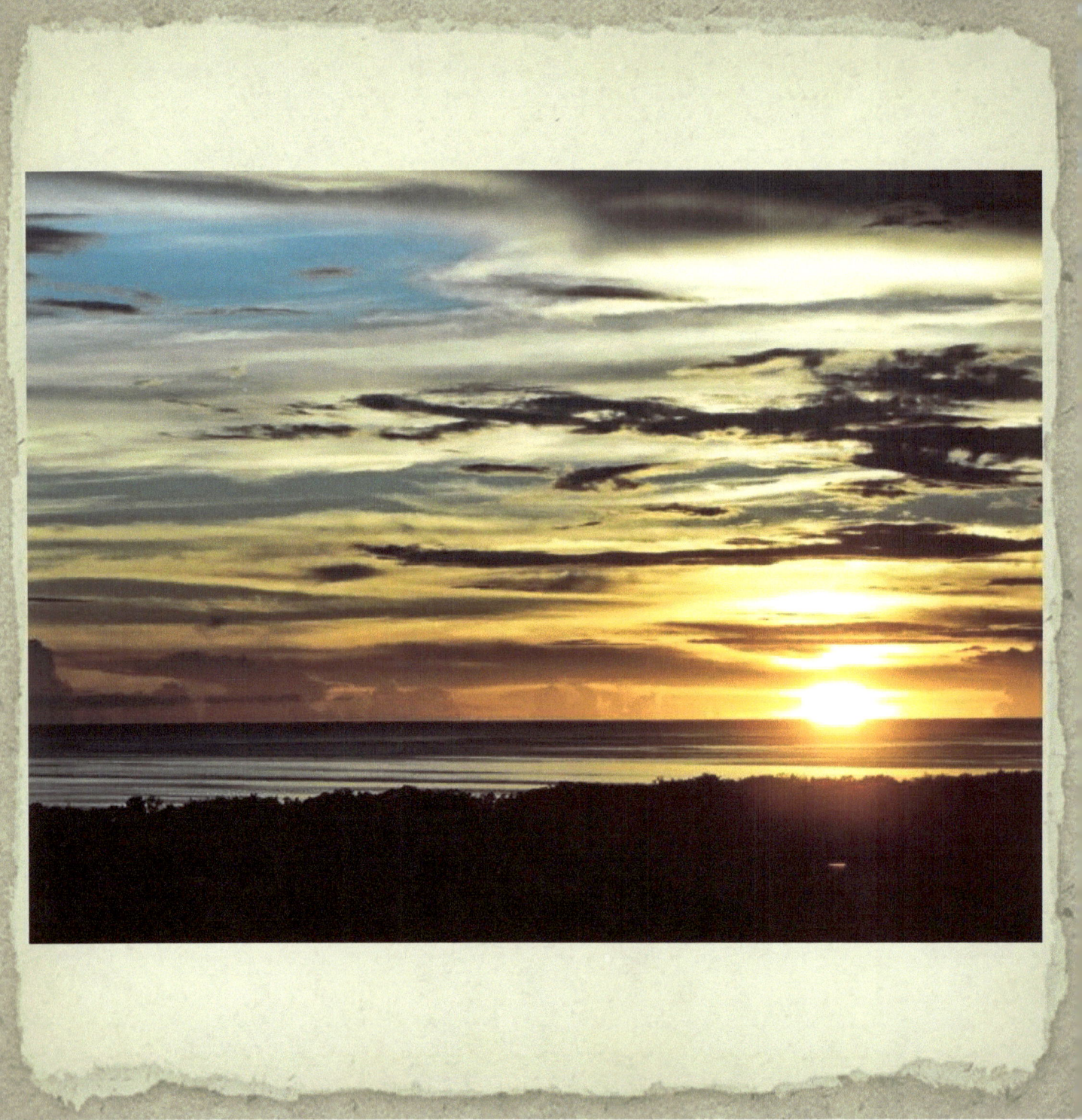

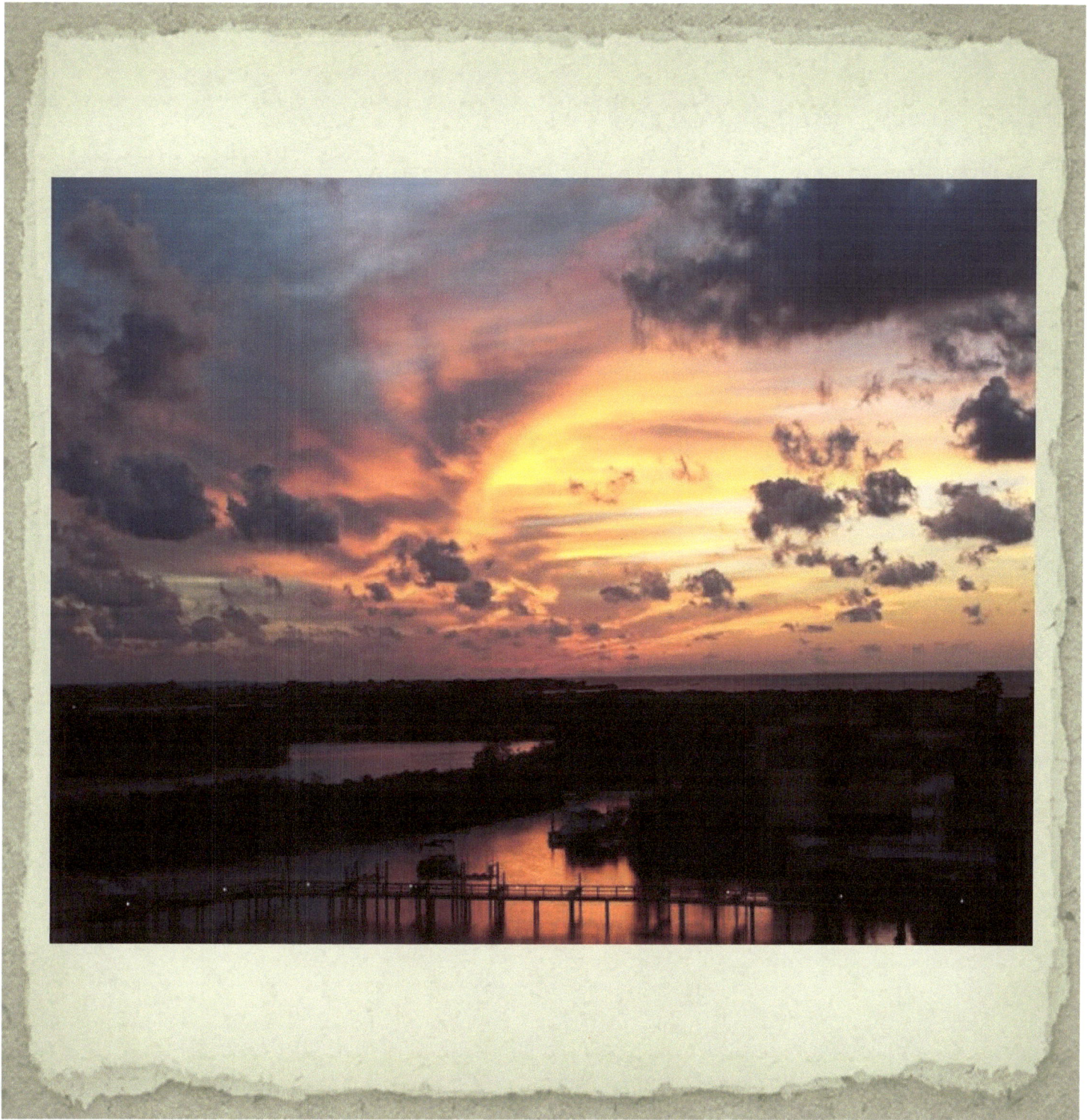

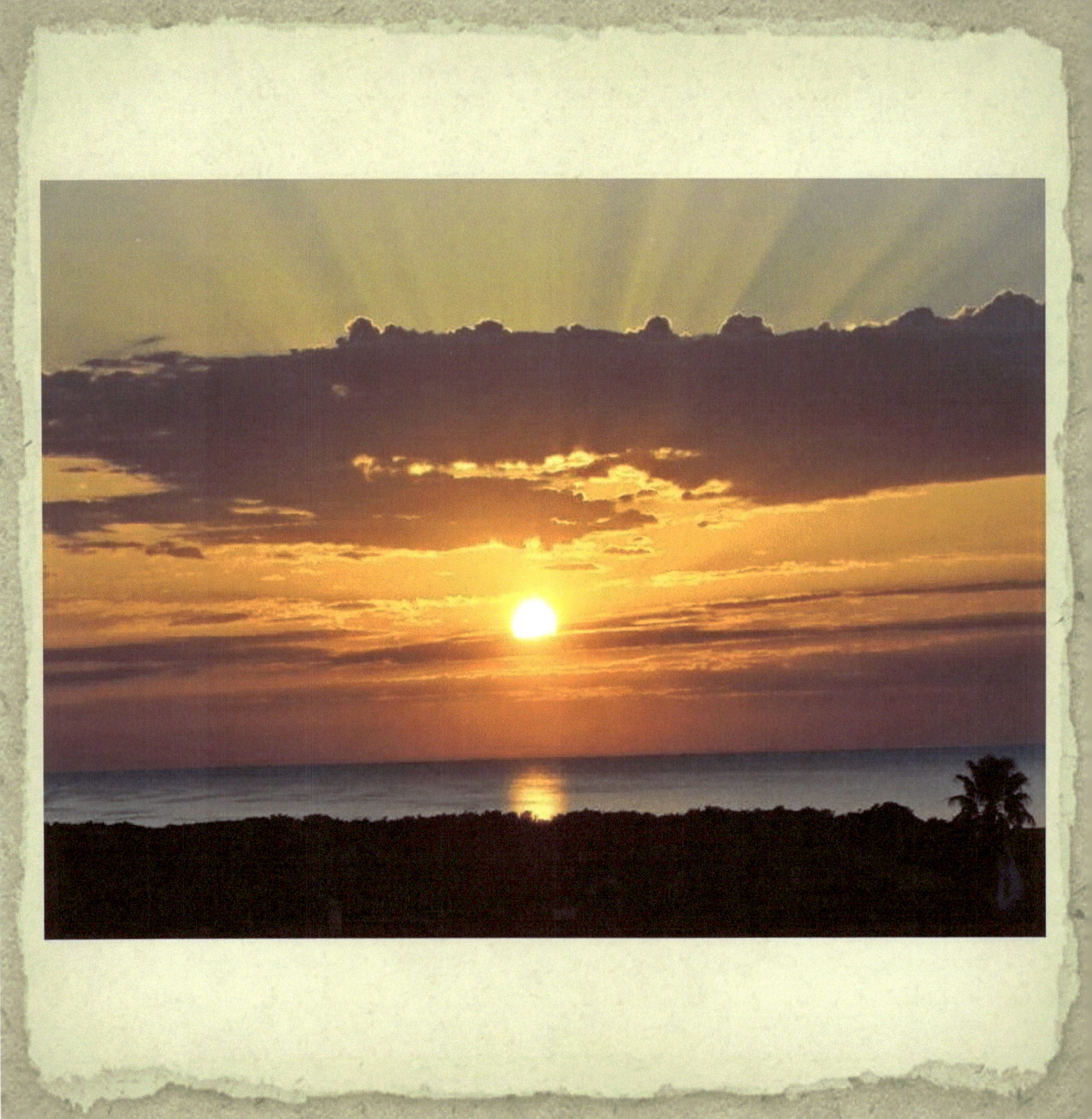

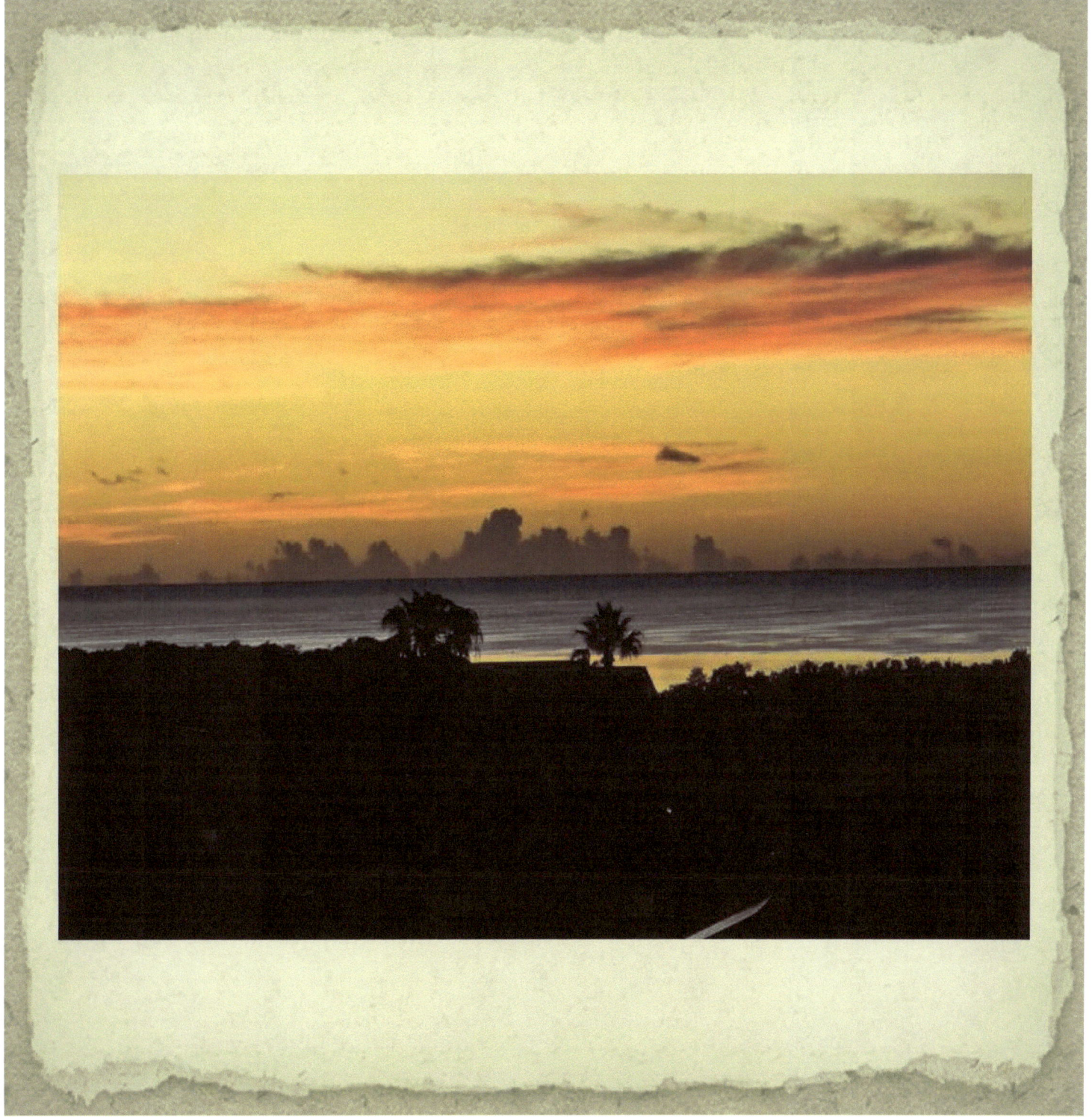

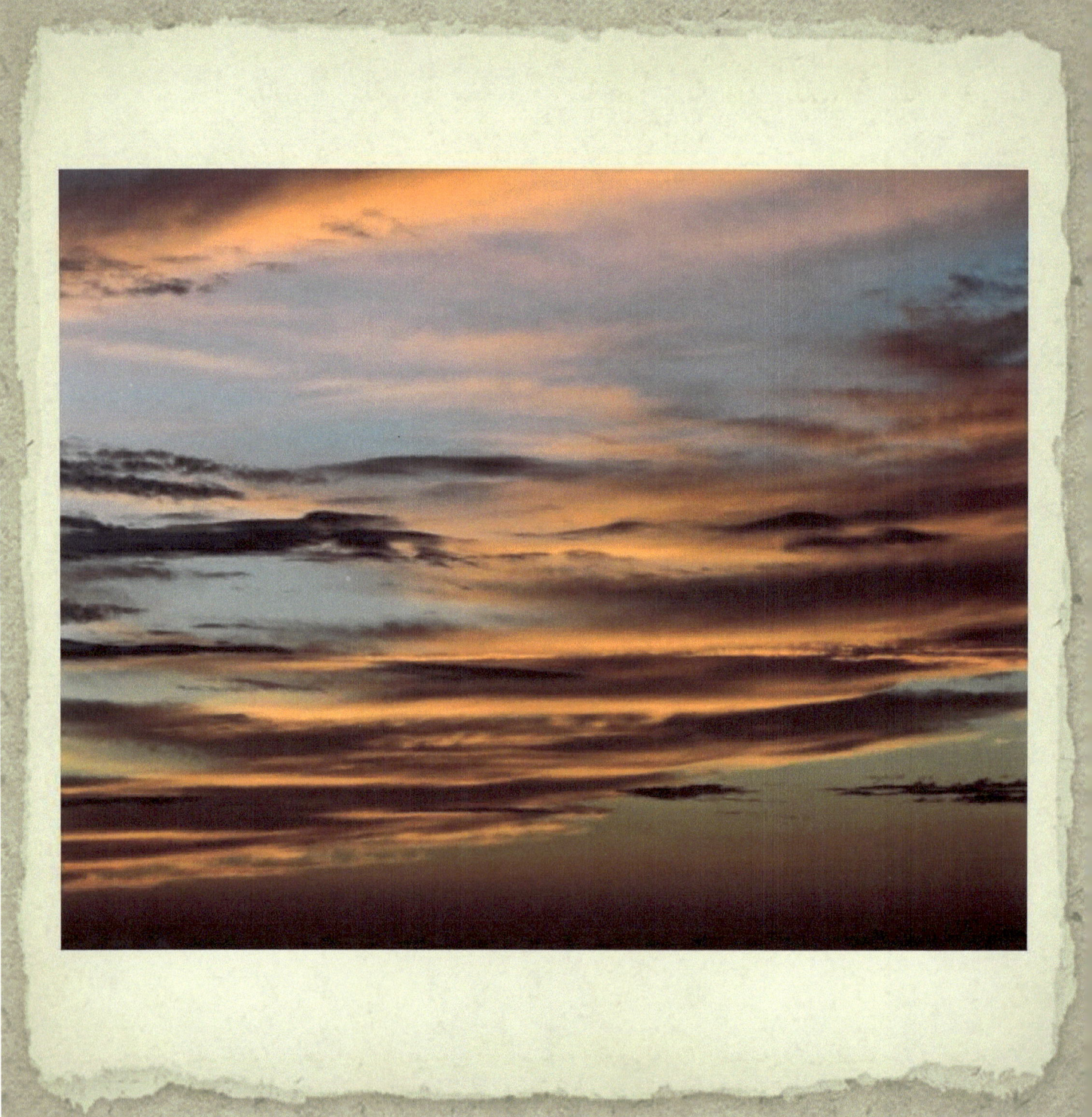

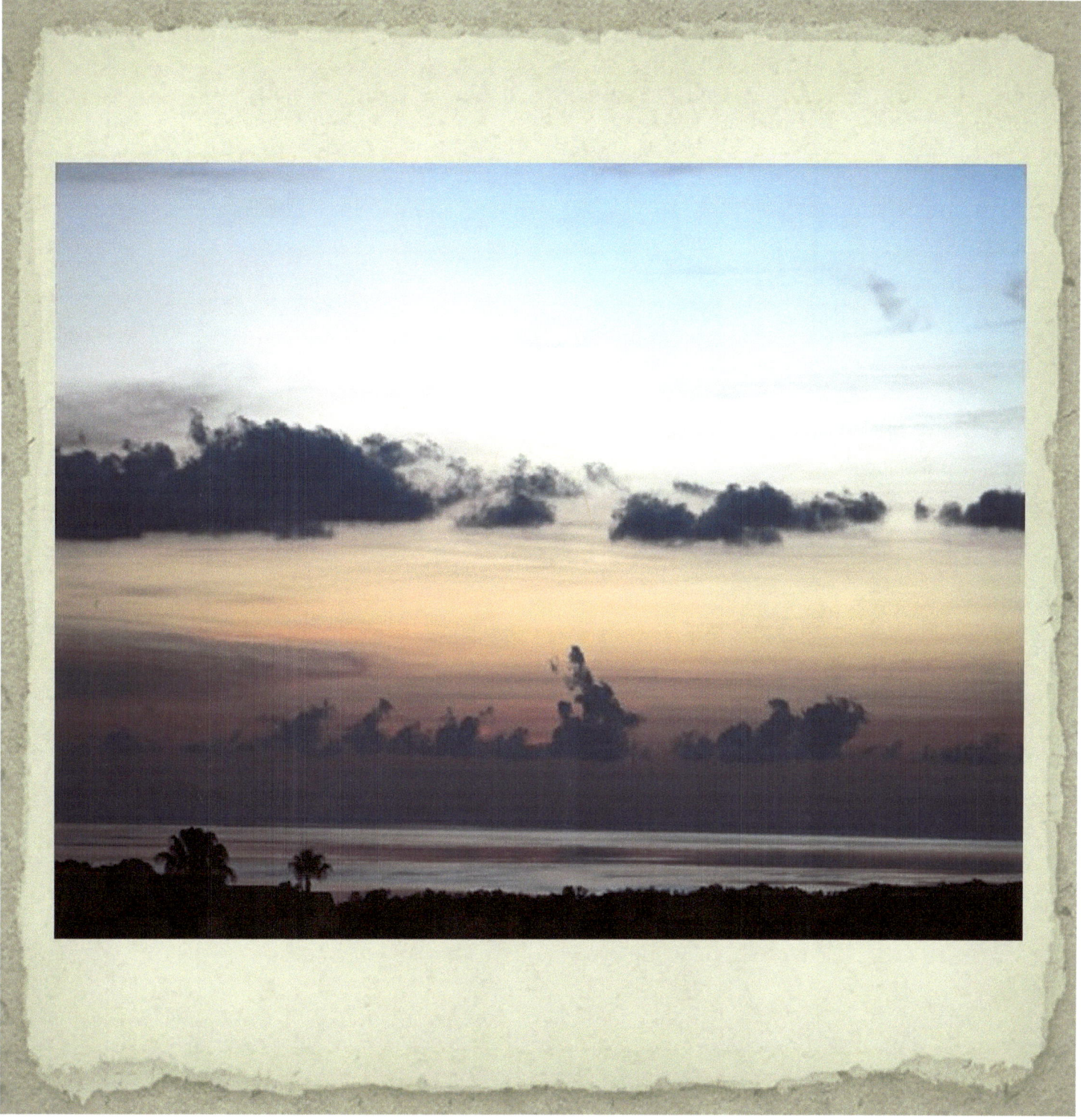

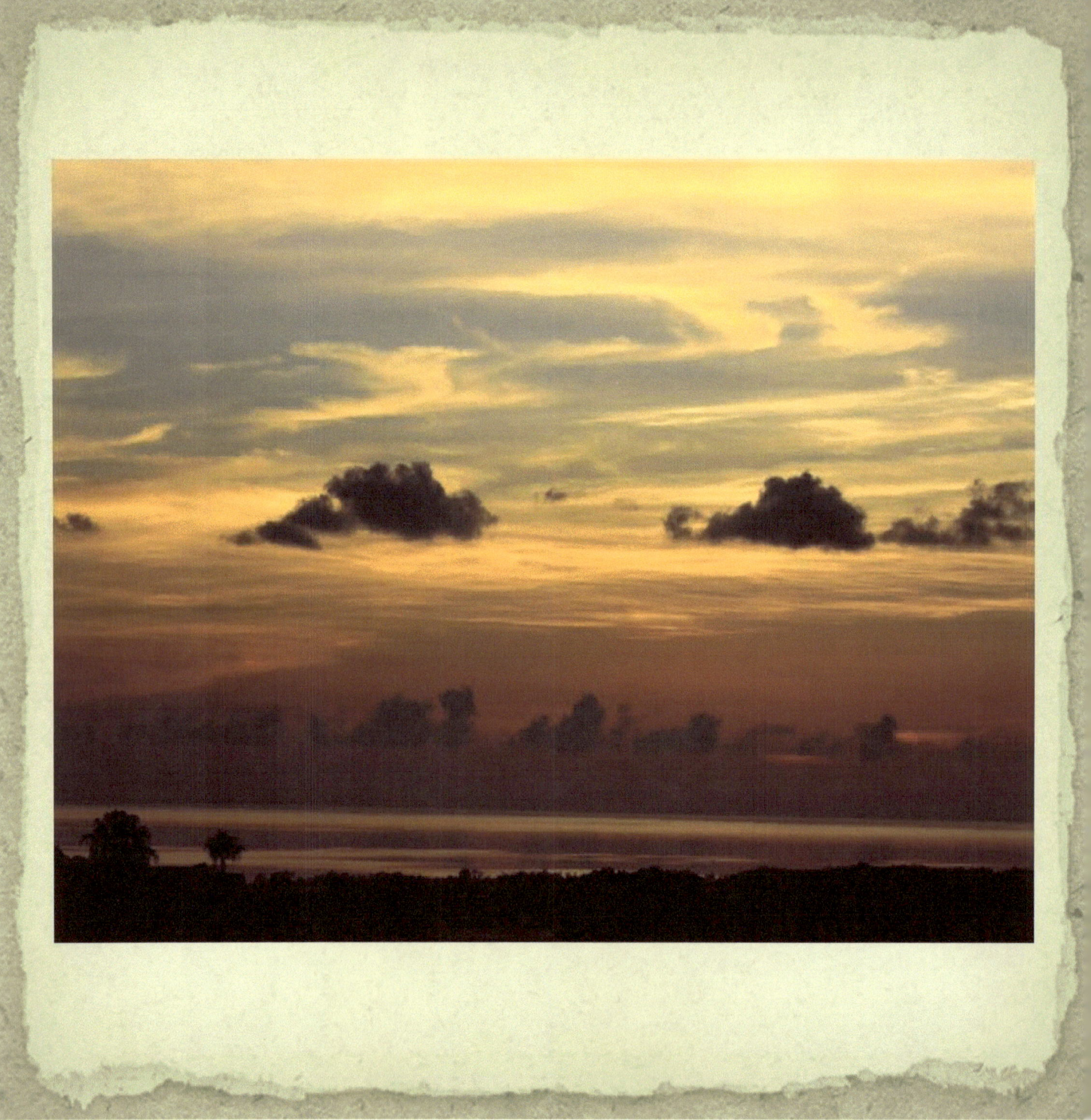

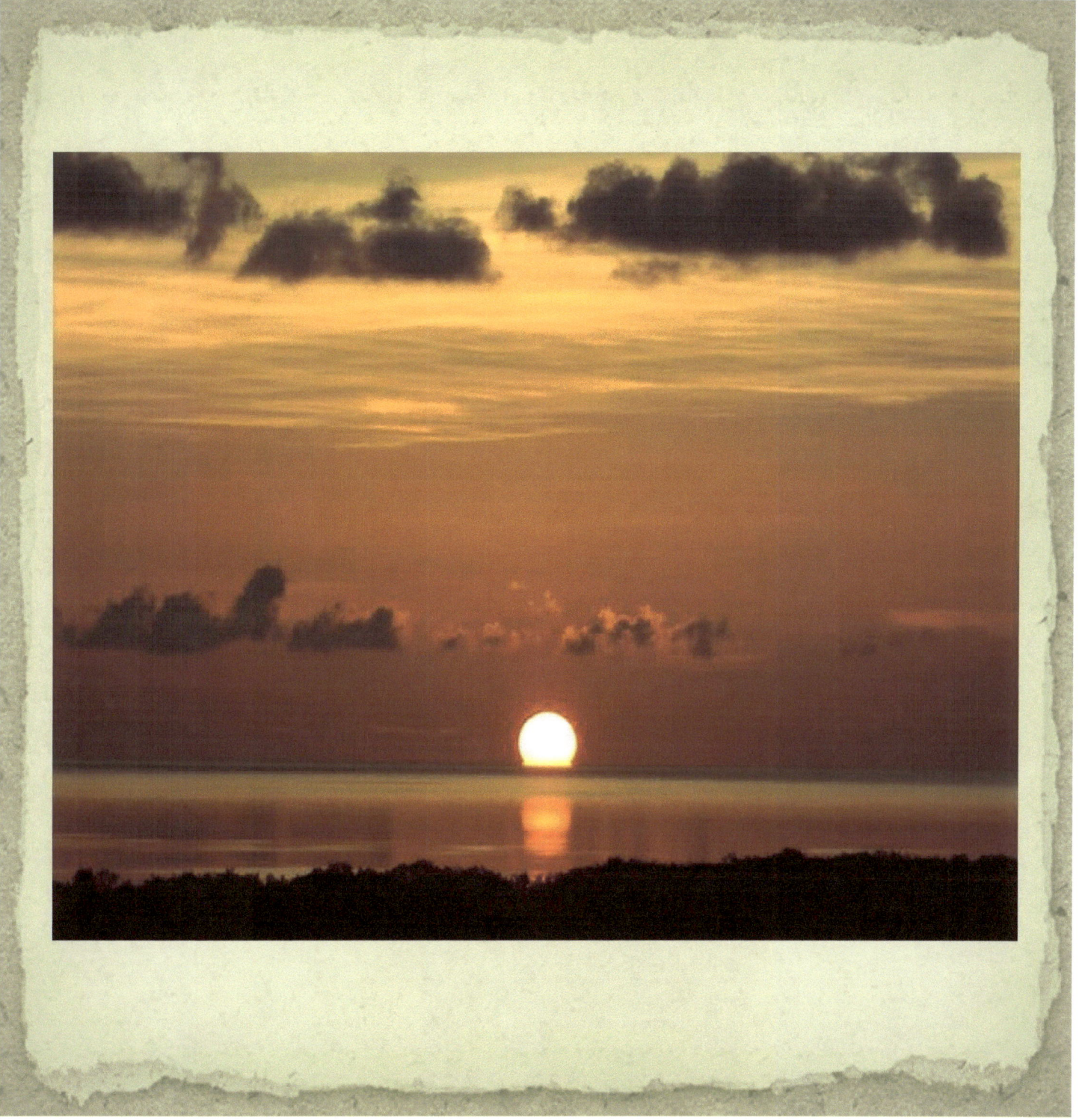

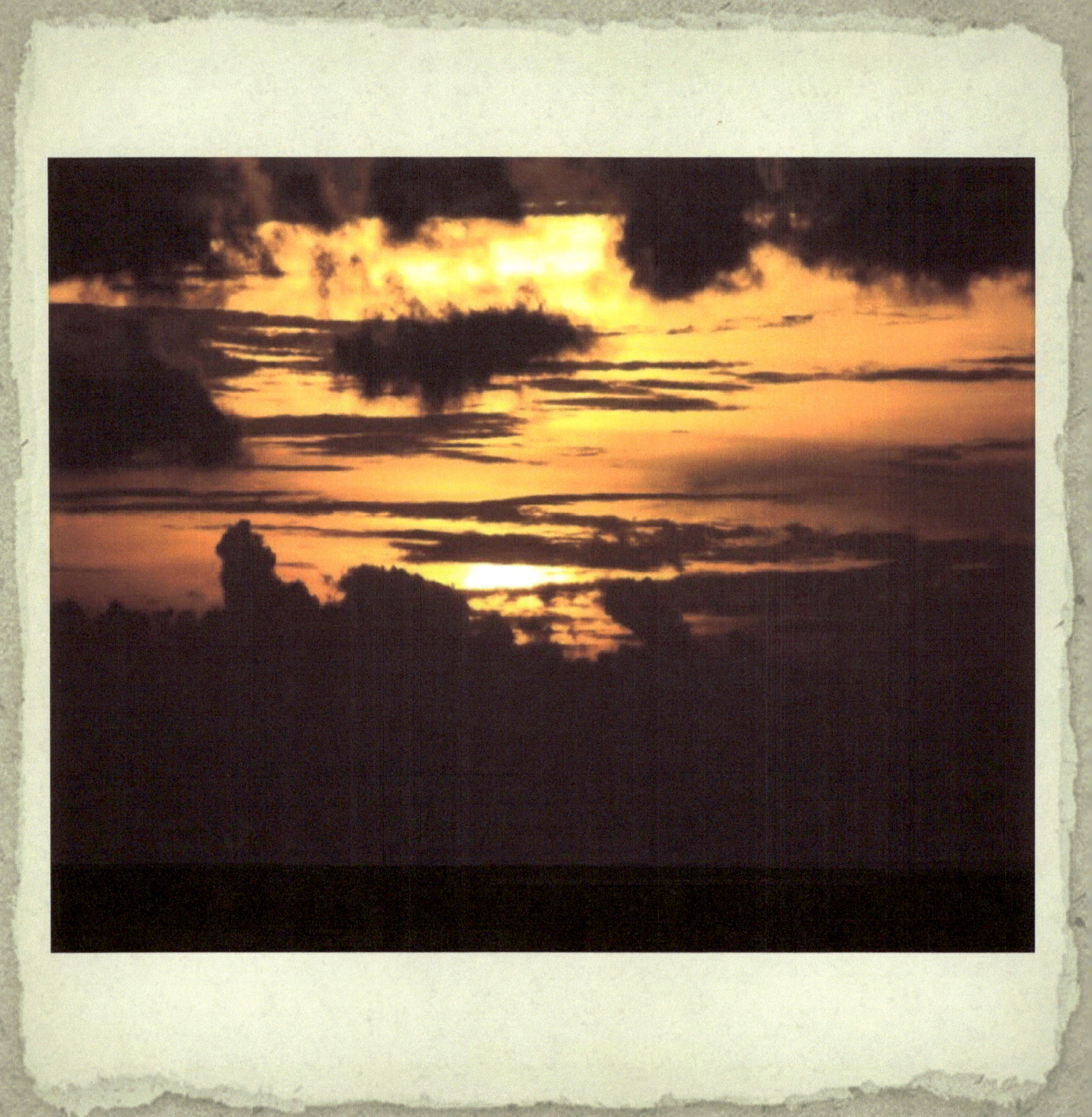

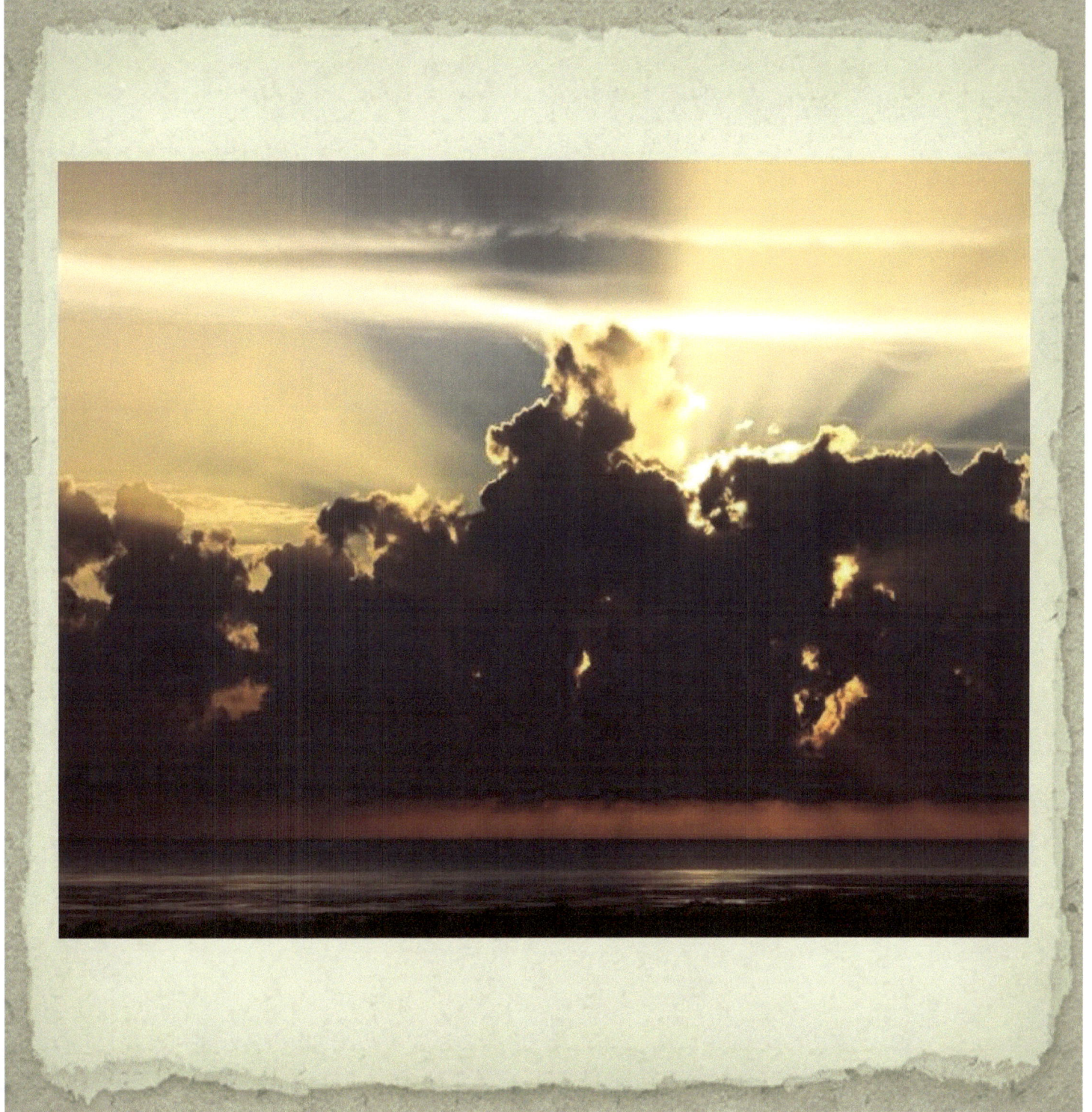

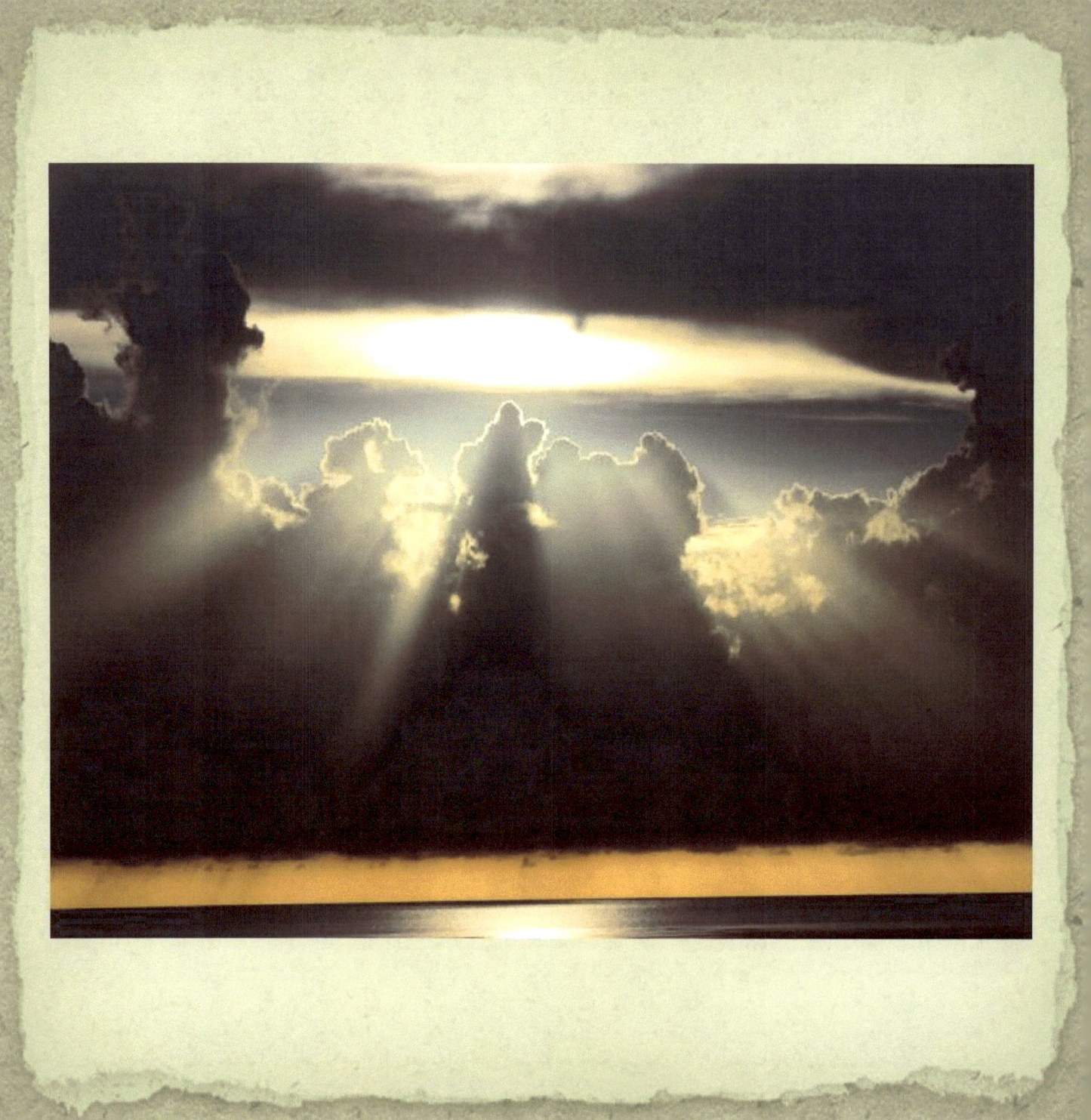

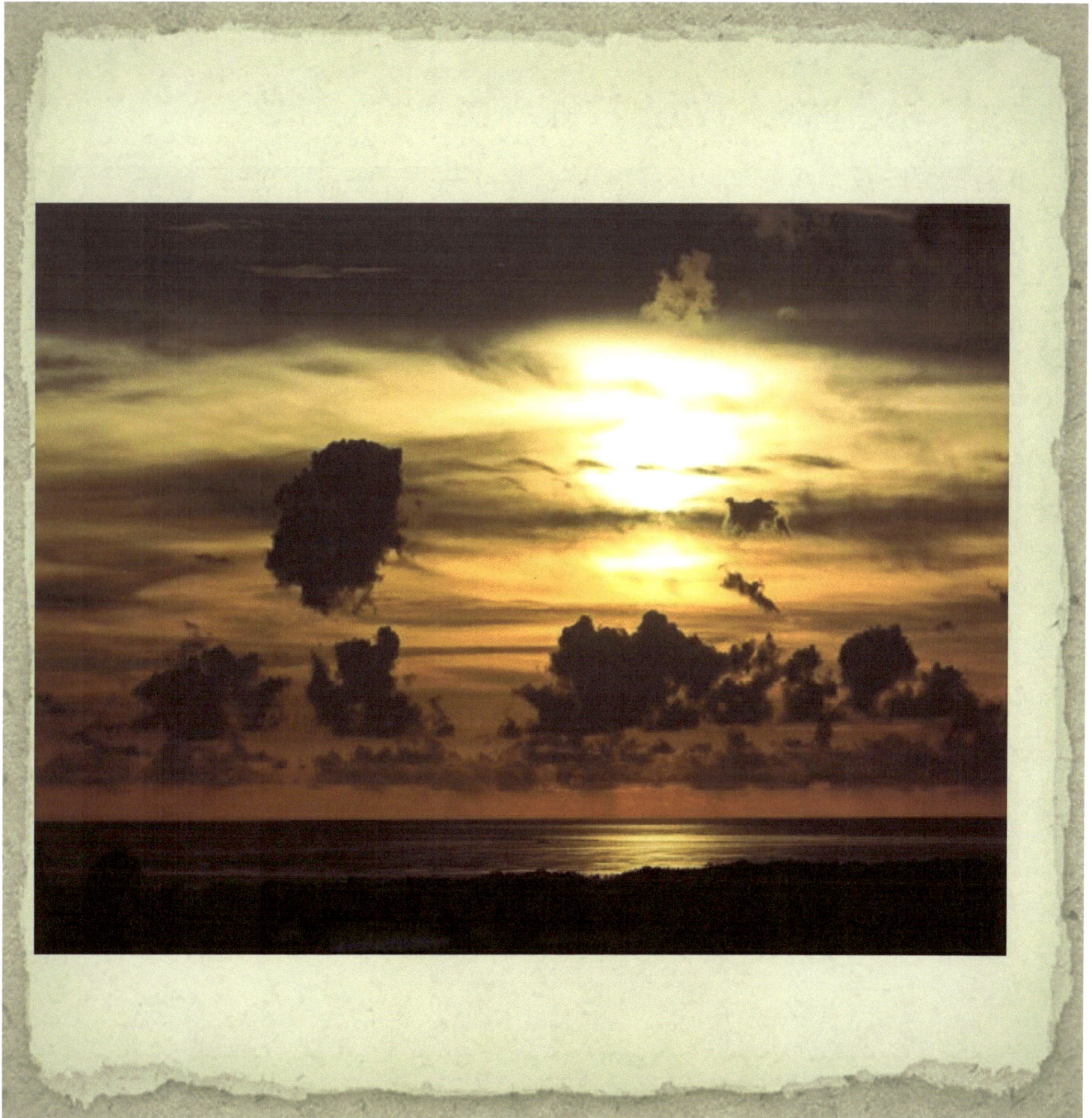

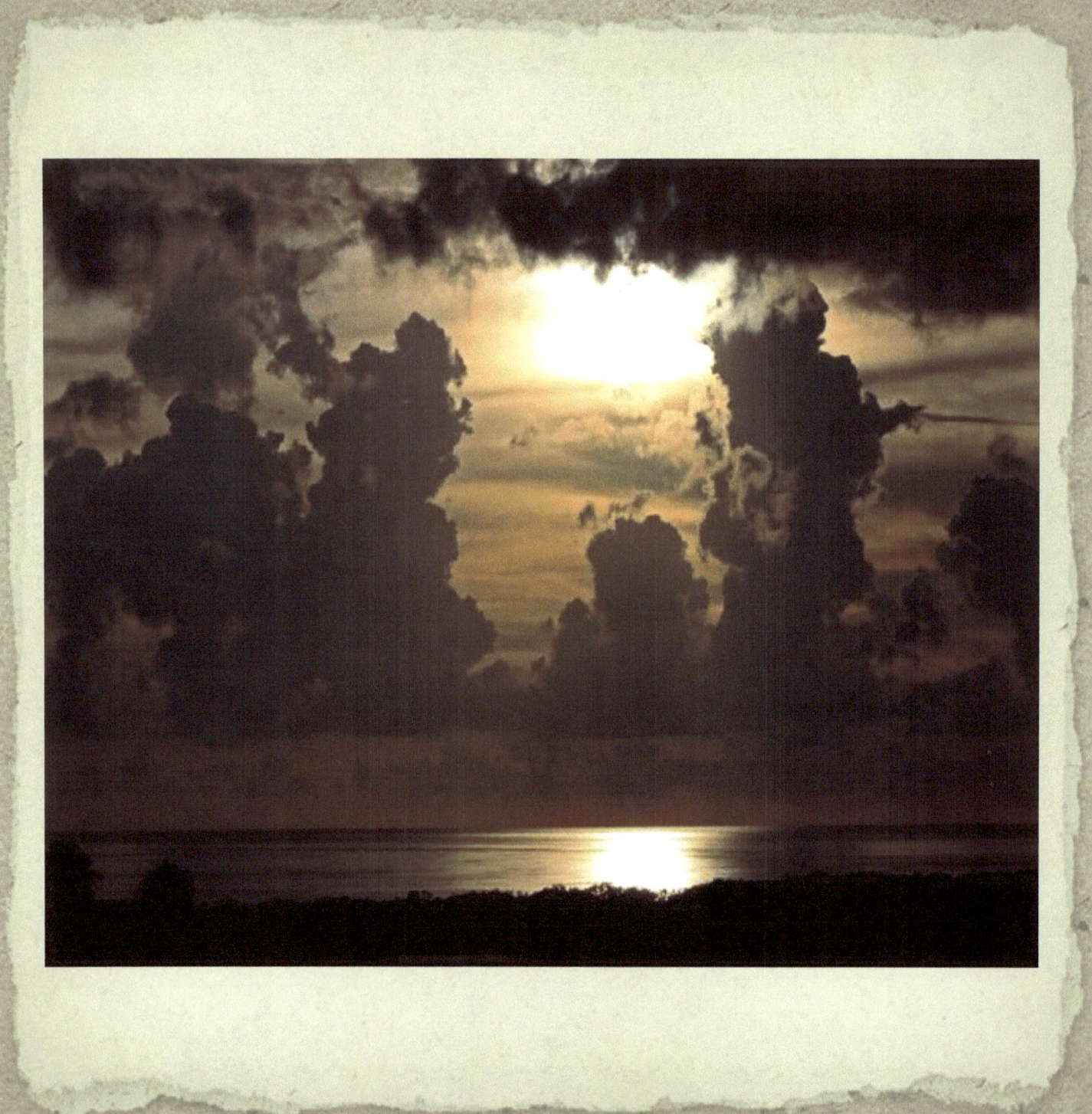

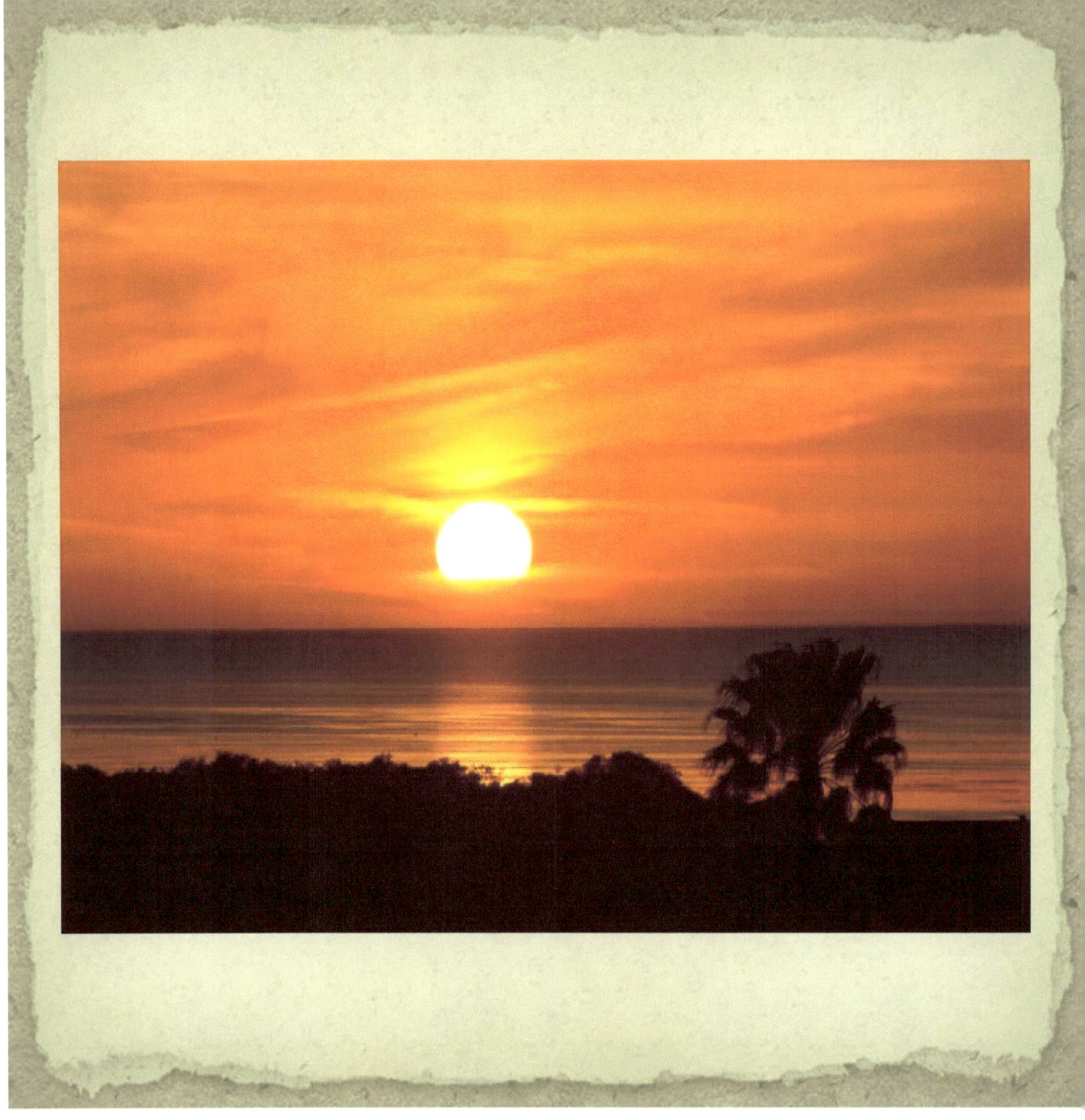

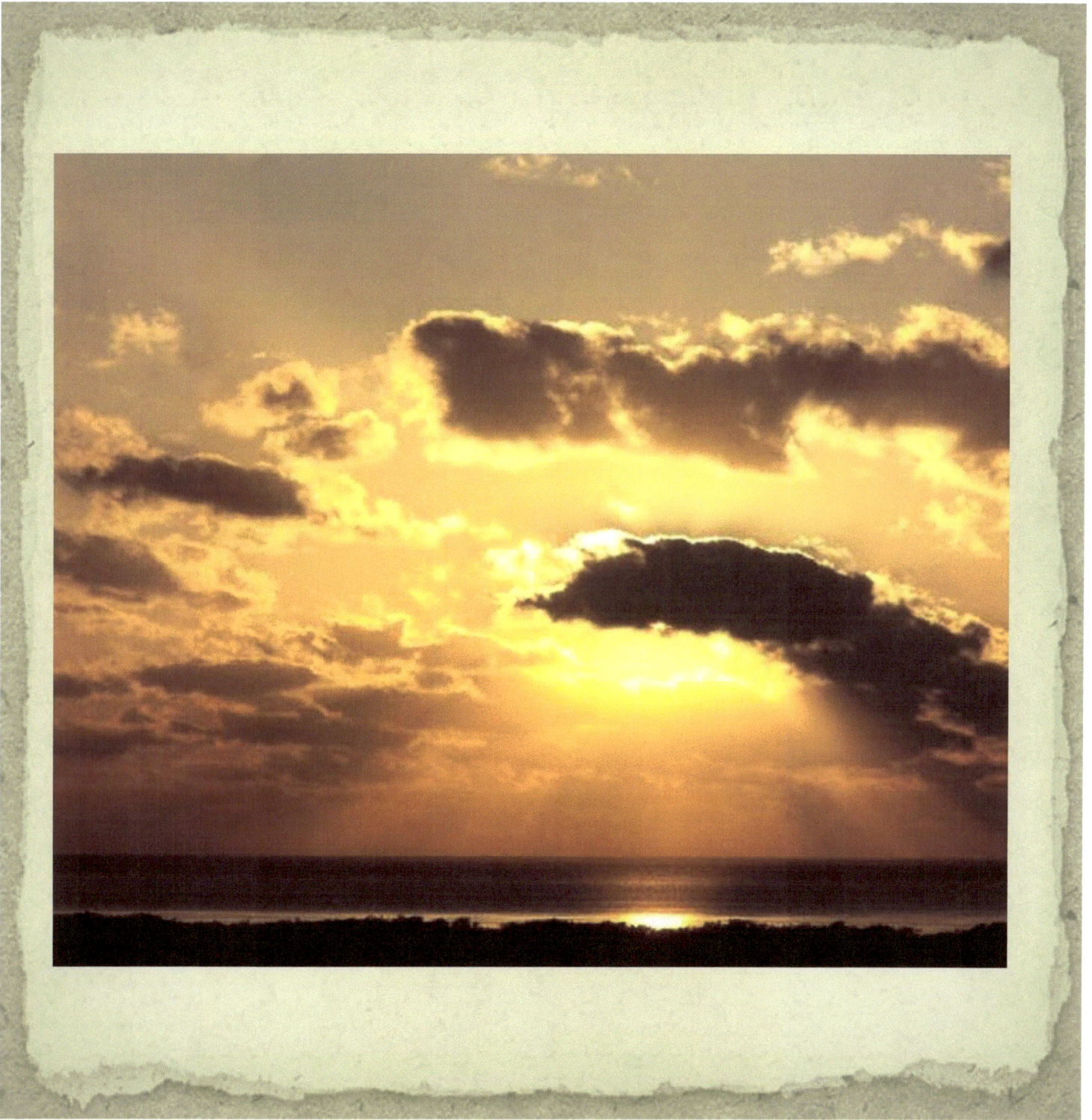

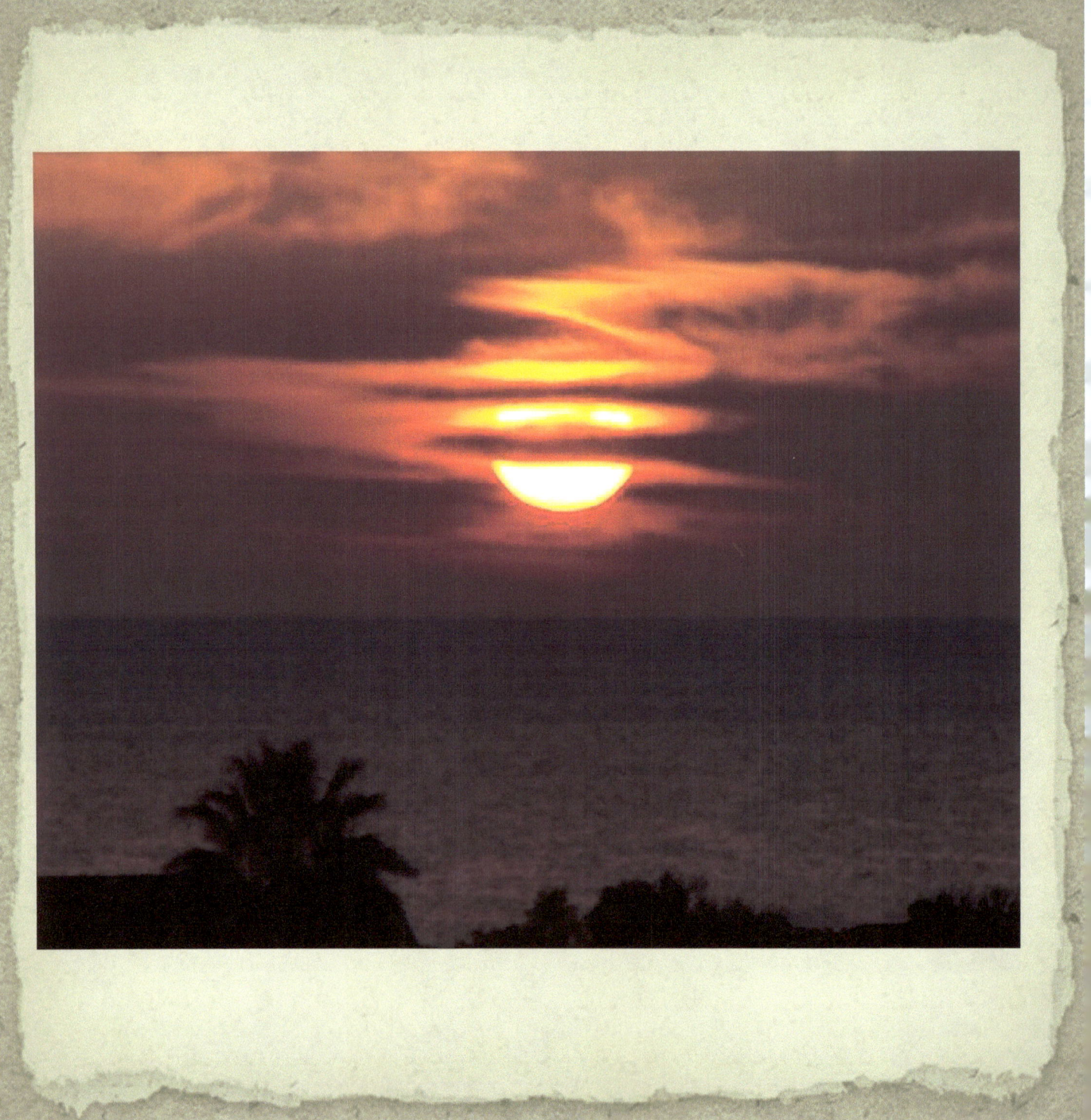

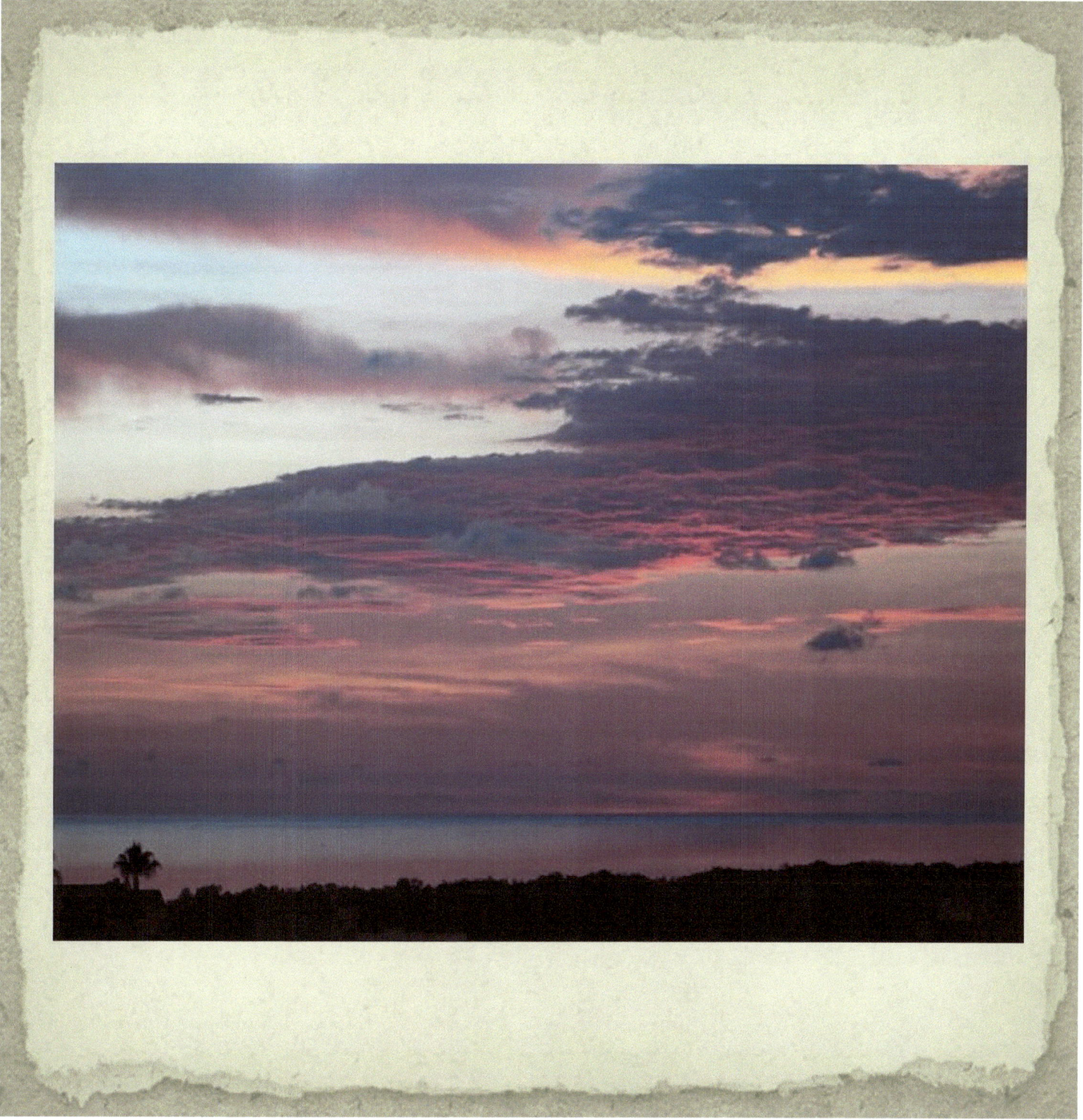

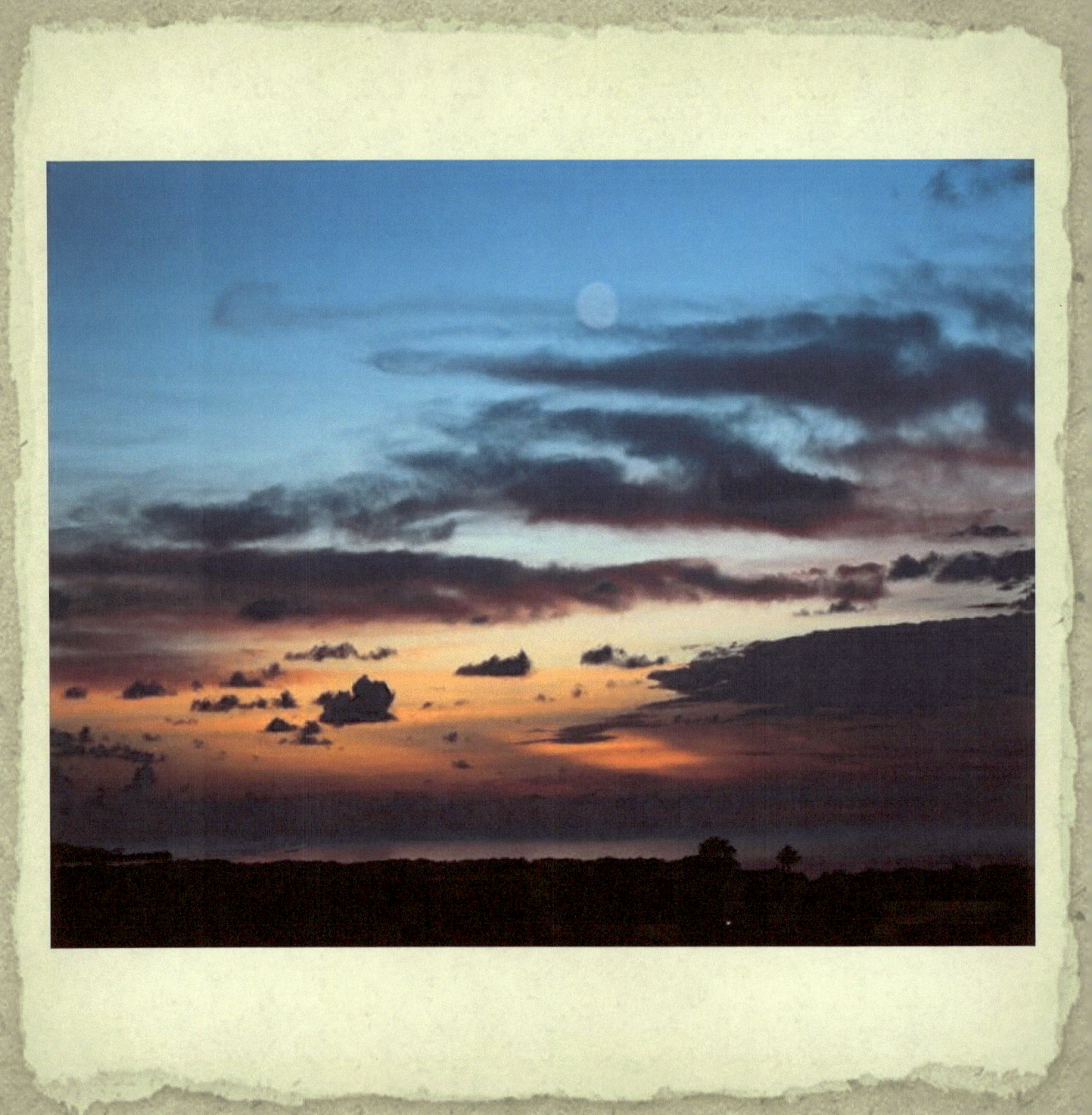

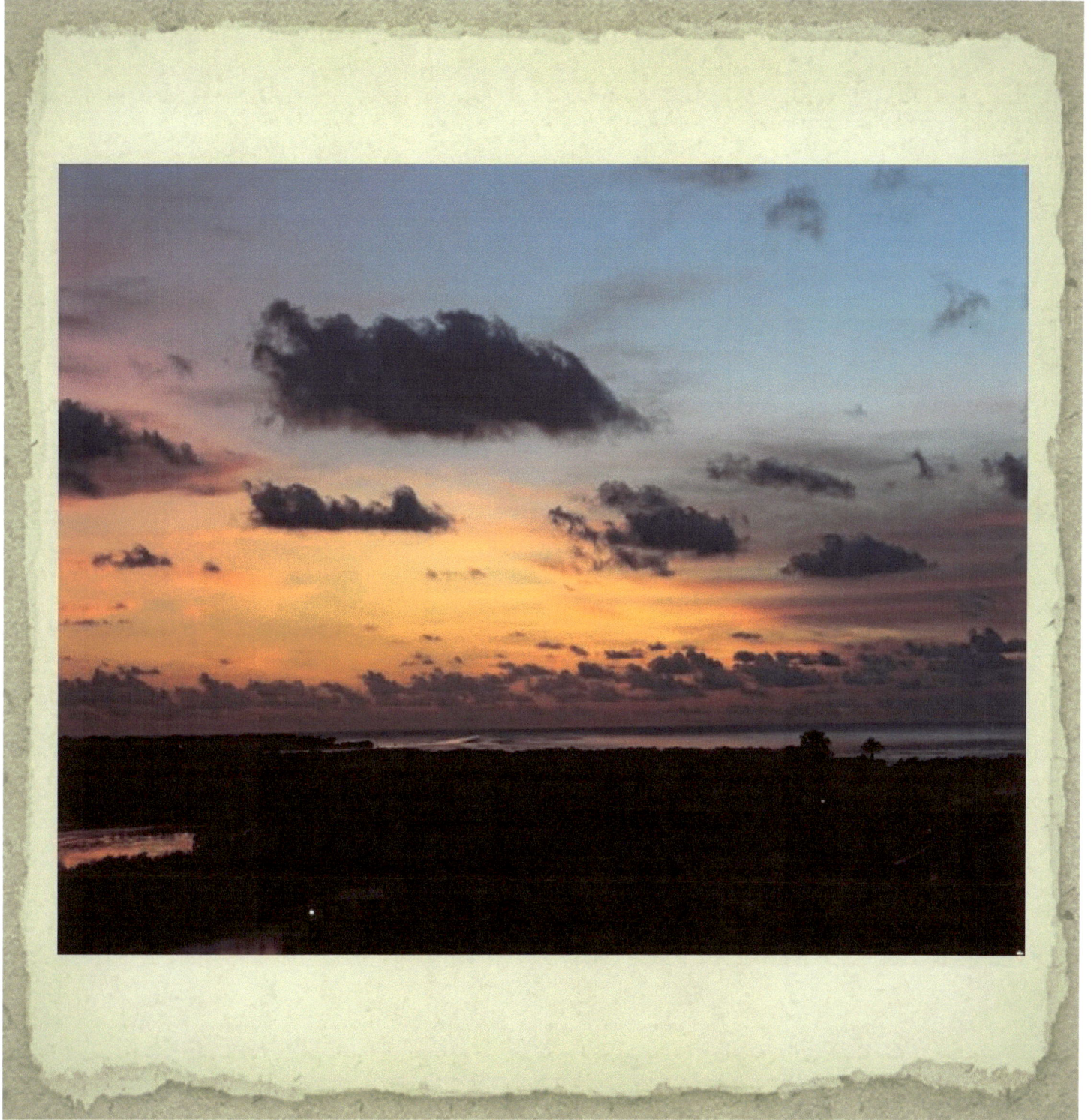

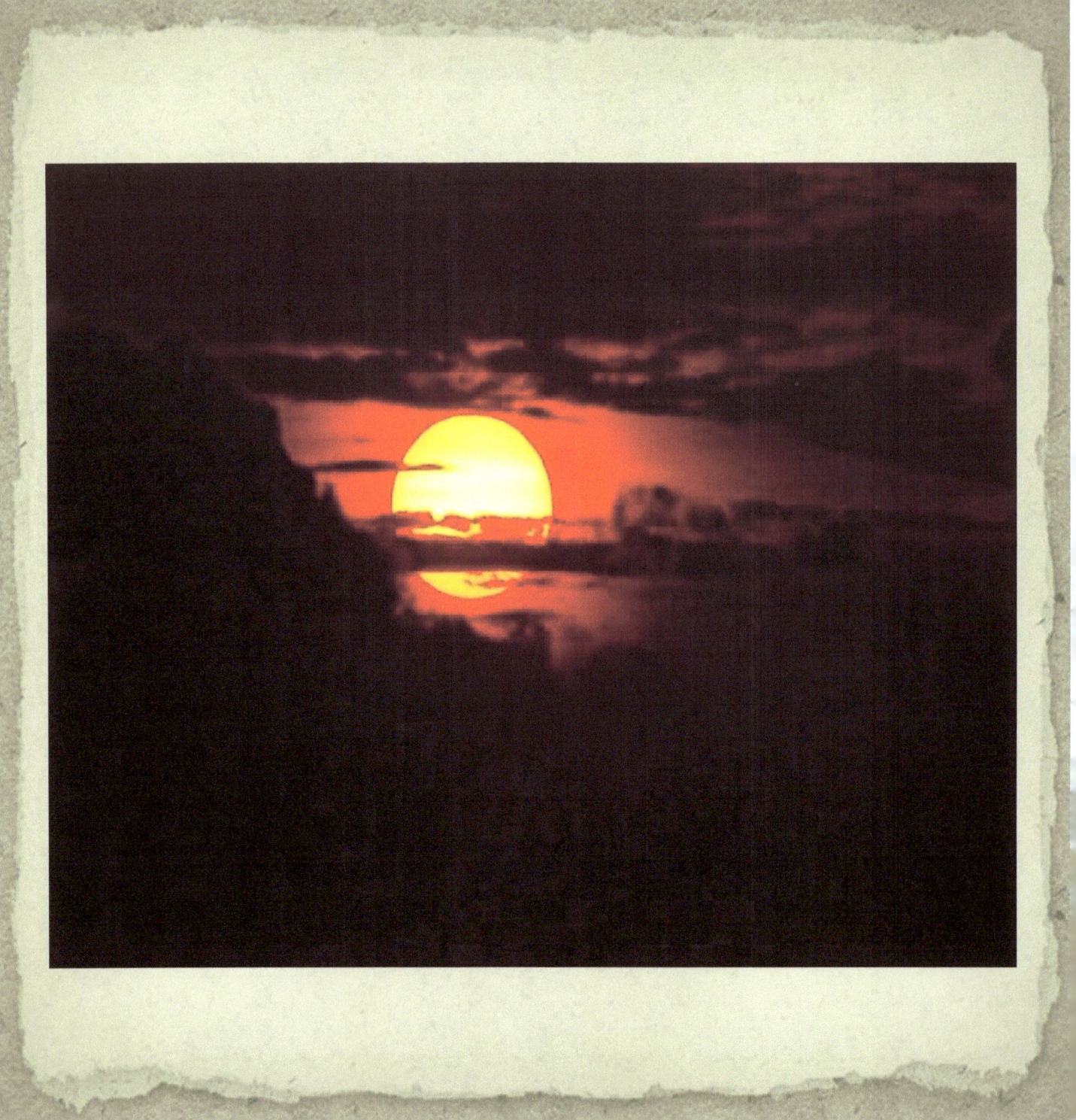

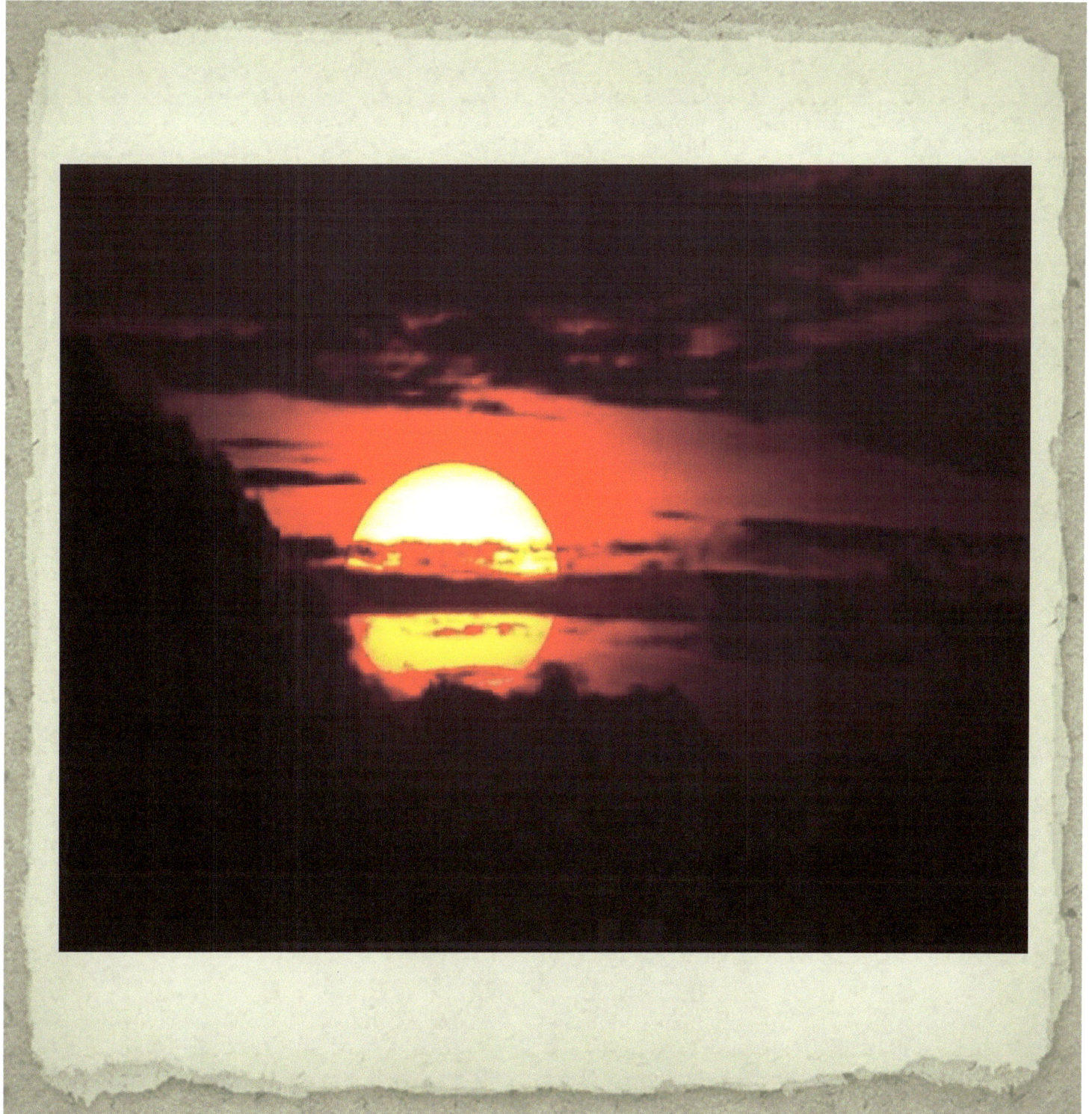

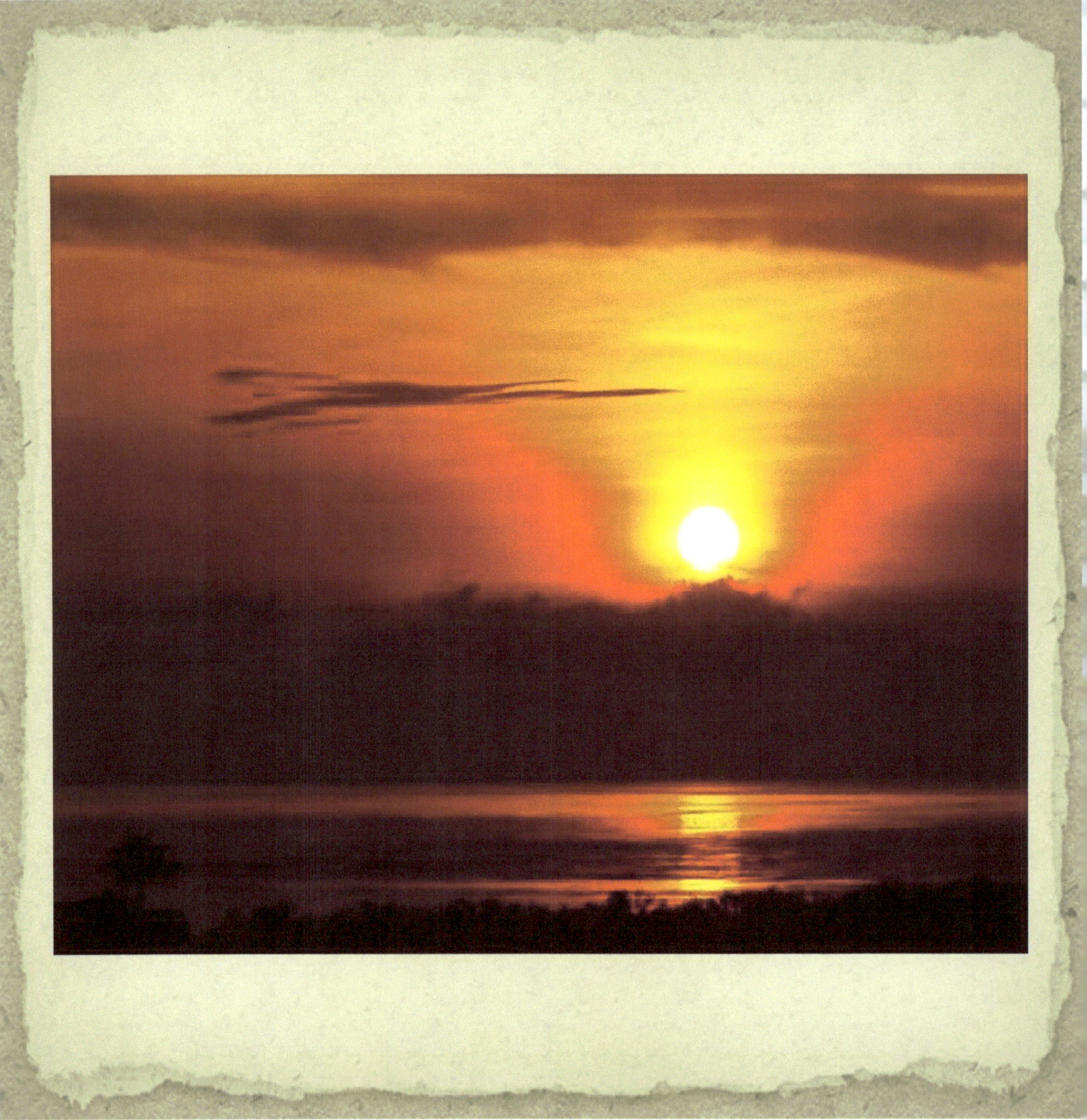

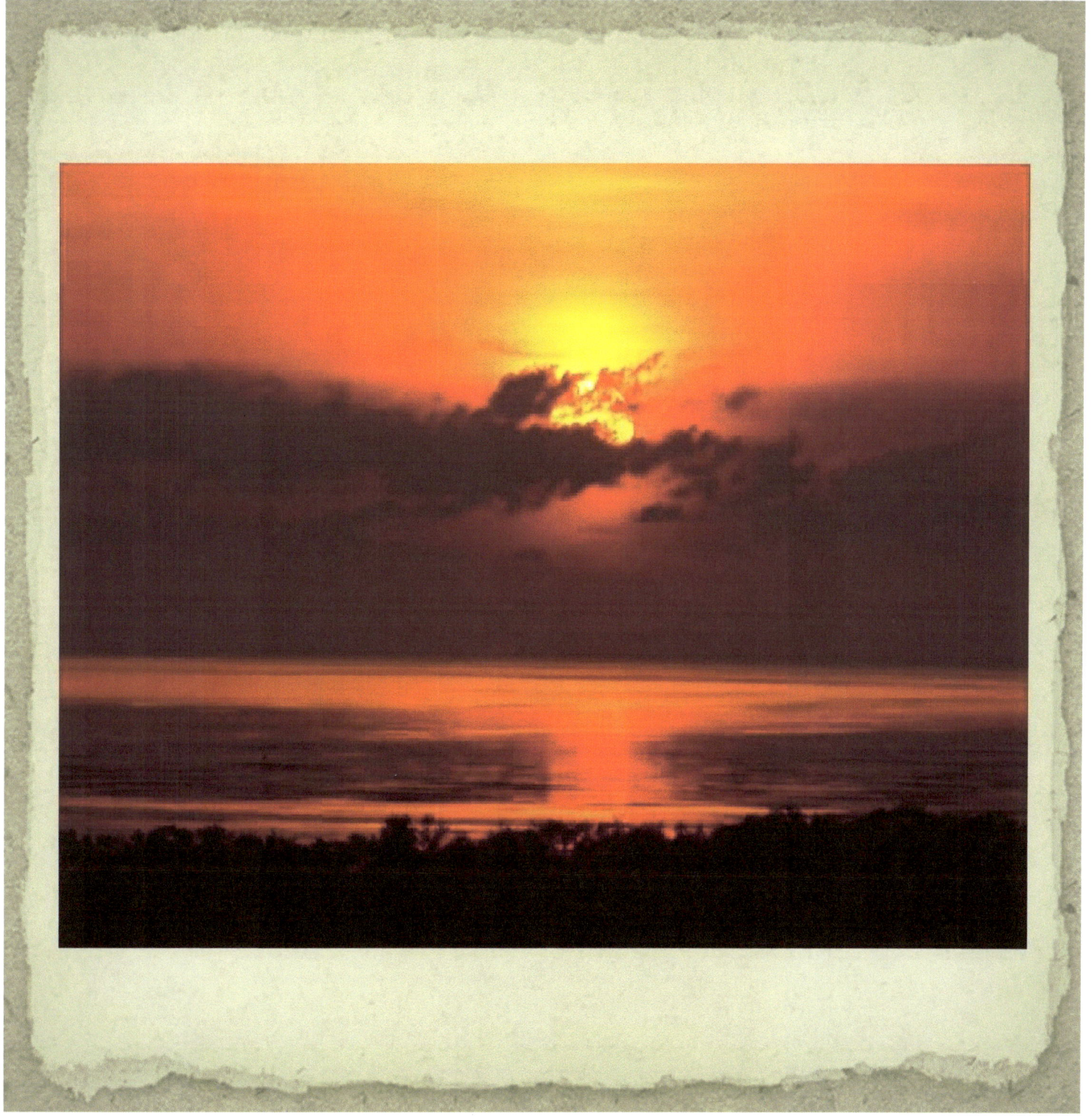

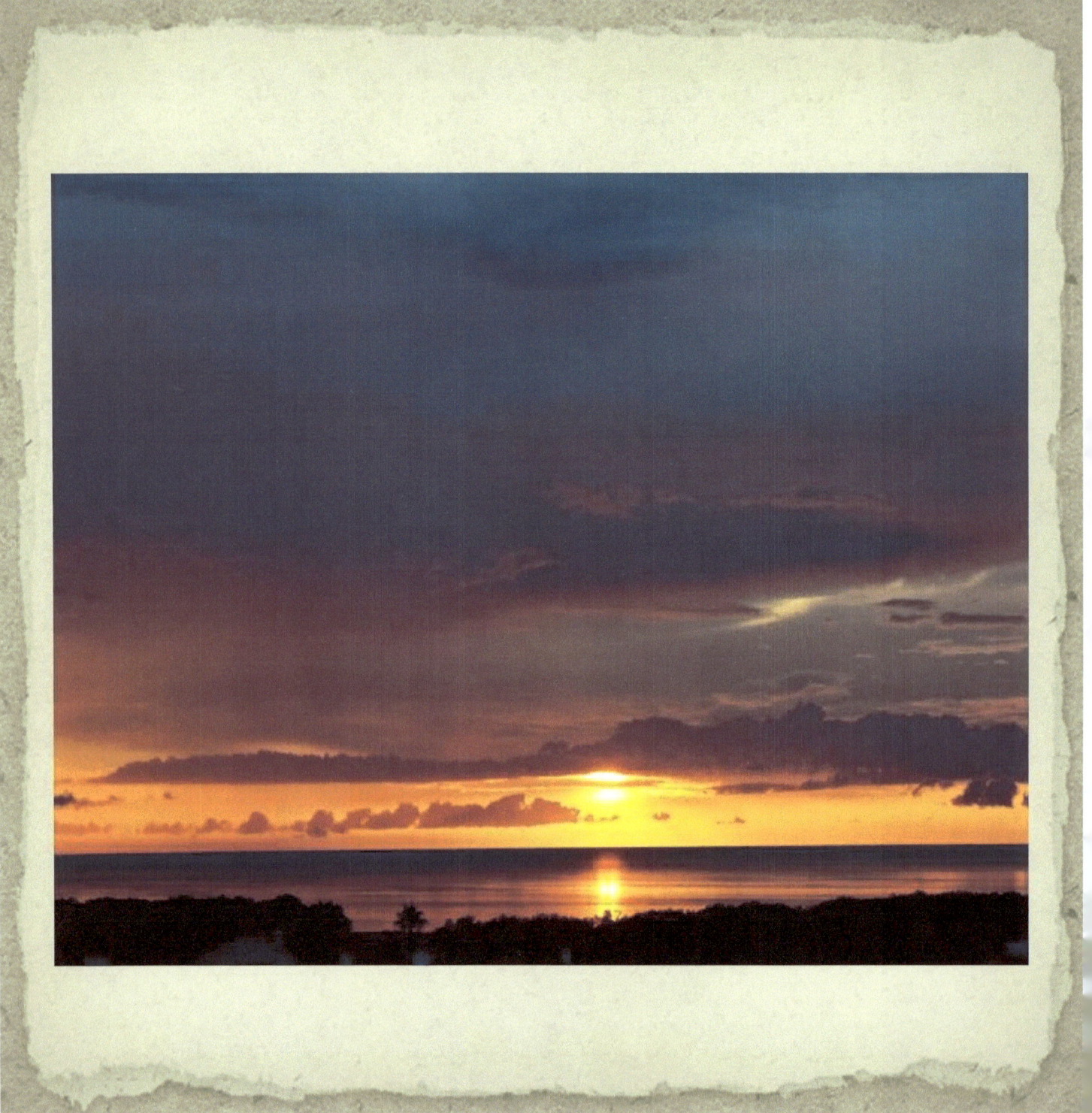

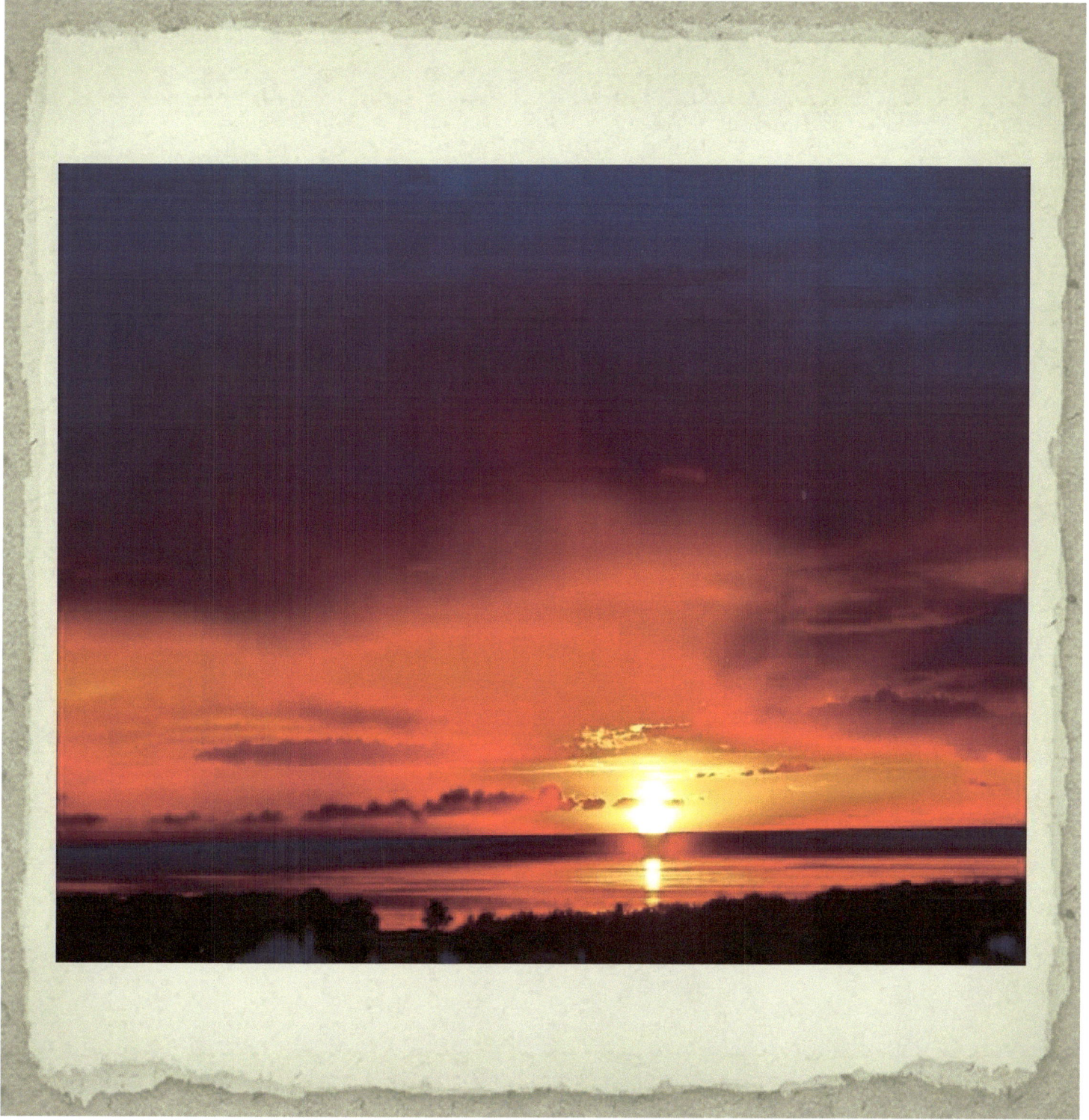

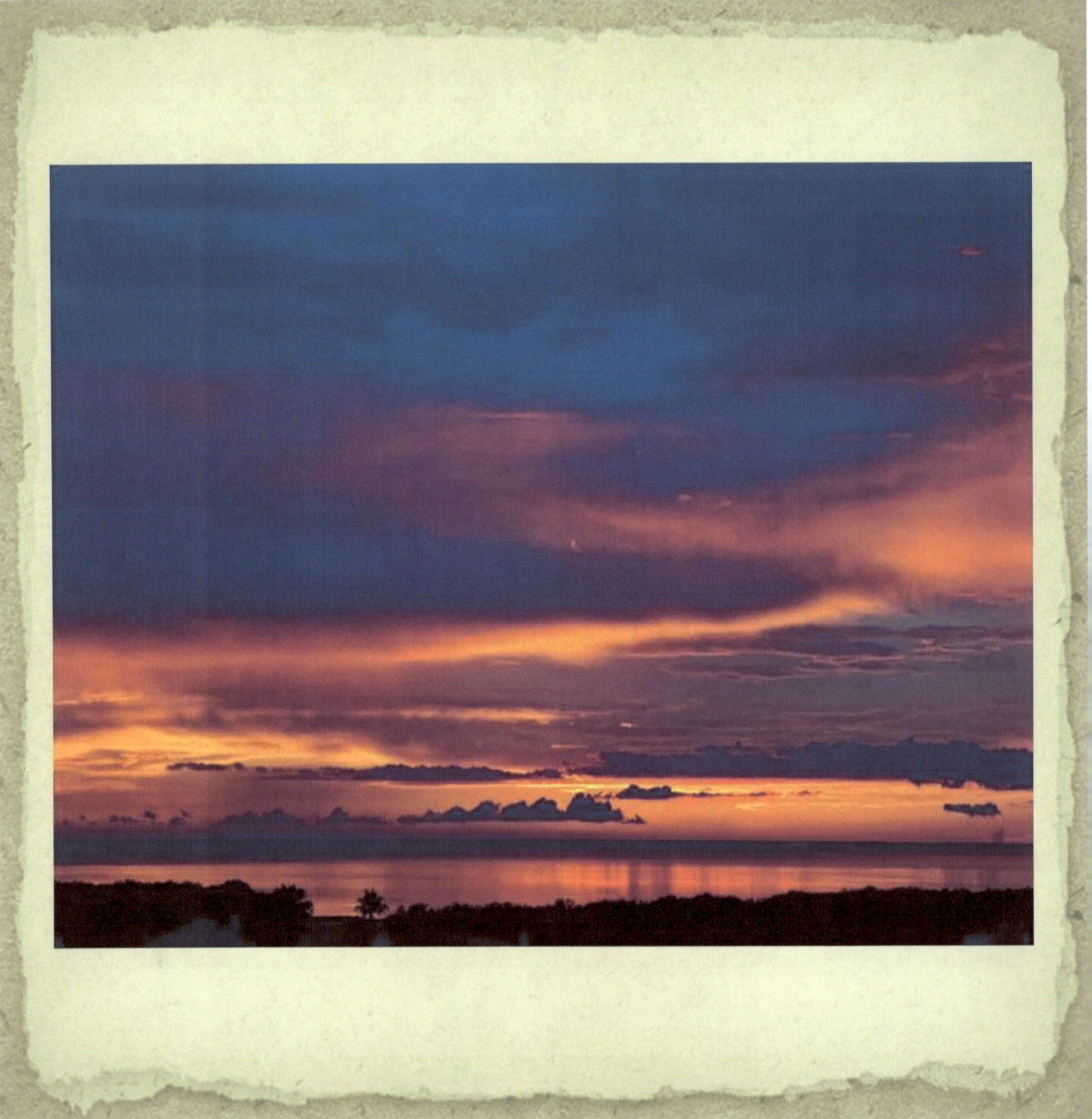

www.ingramcontent.com/pod-product-compliance
Lightning Source LLC
Chambersburg PA
CBHW050814180526
45159CB00004B/1668